Praise for

Ghosts from Our Past: Both Literally and Figuratively: The Study of the Paranormal

"Spectral entities are real—and dangerous. If only I'd taken Drs. Gilbert and Yates's research seriously, I could have saved myself thousands of dollars in out-of-pocket medical expenses."

—*Martin Heiss, former chairman of the Council for Logic and Data*

"Unbelievably absurd."

—*Dr. Harold Filmore, head of the Columbia University Physics Department*

"Rigorously researched and thoroughly entertaining, *Ghosts from Our Past* is a much-needed kick in the pants to the stagnant field of parapsychology. Erin Gilbert and Abby L. Yates give me hope for the future."

—*Christopher Merritt in* American Parapsychology

"An imaginative work of fiction, written by two women I have most definitely never met. Are you recording this? Turn that off."

—*New York City's Mayor Bradley*

"A fascinating journey through the spirit kingdom. *Ghosts from Our Past* is an eye-opening study that deserves a permanent place on every ghost hunter's bookshelf."

—*Maureen Kemp, author of* Kemp's Spectral Field Guide

"5 stars. Arrived on time. Good condition."

—*Amazon.com review*

Also by Erin Gilbert and Abby L. Yates

A Glimpse into the Unknown: A Journey into a Portal;
Catching Sight of the Other Dimension: Discovering the Undiscoverable:
A Curiosity Piqued and Peaked

Ghosts from Our Past

Both Literally and Figuratively: The Study of the Paranormal

ERIN GILBERT, PH.D., M.S., AND ABBY L. YATES, PH.D.,

WITH ANDREW SHAFFER

THREE RIVERS PRESS • NEW YORK

Published in the United States by Three Rivers Press, an imprint of the Crown Publishing Group, a division of Penguin Random House LLC, New York.
www.crownpublishing.com

Three Rivers Press and the Tugboat design are registered trademarks of Penguin Random House LLC.

Published simultaneously in the United Kingdom by Ebury Press, a division of Penguin Random House, London.

Photography credits appear on page 217.

Library of Congress Cataloging-in-Publication Data
Names: Gilbert, Erin, author. | Yates, Abby L., author. | Shaffer, Andrew, 1978- author.
Title: Ghosts from our past : both literally and figuratively : the study of the paranormal / Erin Gilbert, Abby L. Yates and Andrew Shaffer.
Description: First edition. | New York : Three Rivers Press, [2016] | "Authors" Erin Gilbert and Abby L. Yates are fictitious characters played in the film by Kristen Wiig and Melissa McCarthy.
Identifiers: LCCN 2016004068| ISBN 9781101906002 (paperback) | ISBN 9781101906095 (electronic)
Subjects: LCSH: Ghostbusters (Motion picture : 2016)—Miscellanea. | Ghosts—Humor. | BISAC: FICTION / Media Tie-In. | HUMOR / Form / Parodies.
Classification: LCC PN1997.G44535 G55 2016 | DDC 791.43/72—dc23 LC record available at http://lccn.loc.gov/2016004068

ISBN 978-1-101-90600-2
eBook ISBN 978-1-101-90609-5

Printed in the United States of America

Book design by Chad Tomlinson
Illustrations by Steven Salerno
Cover: Motion Picture Artwork and Photos TM & © 2016 Columbia Pictures Industries, Inc. All Rights Reserved.

10 9 8 7 6 5 4 3 2 1

First Edition

"We do not know what happens when we die, or where we go to, or how we get there. And if we can 'come back'—in the spiritualistic sense—we do not know how that occurs either."

—*Ghost hunter Harry Price*

"We know."

—*Erin Gilbert and Abby L. Yates*

A Note to Readers

Because this book is intended for a general audience,
we have made every attempt to use the smallest words possible.
Where specialized paranormal terminology is unavoidable,
we've defined it in the dictionary at the back of the book.

You're welcome.

Contents

New Foreword

As chairman of the Council for Logic and Data, I debunked dozens of paranormal pranksters over the years. Remember the famous episode of *The Tonight Show* where the skeptic exposed Uri Geller's hands-free spoon bending as a stage trick? That wasn't me. It was James Randi. But whenever he wasn't available, the networks used to ring up ol' Marty Heiss. No one's called me in a while—someone obviously forgot to pass along my number to Jimmy Fallon.

Anyway, I thought I'd seen just about everything . . . and then along come the Ghostbusters.

At the CLD's annual nondenominational winter holiday office party last year, I received a copy of *Ghosts from Our Past* as a white elephant gift. Everyone had a good laugh at it—and that was just from reading the synopsis aloud.

Later that night, while nursing a bottle of eggnog by the fireplace at my home on the Upper West Side, I casually flipped through the massive tome. *Ghosts from Our Past* wasn't high literature, although it may have been written while in that state of mind. Purportedly a work of serious scientific inquiry, the personal asides, run-on sentences, and numerous digressions distracted from whatever points the authors were attempting to make. My laughter soon gave way to secondhand embarrassment.

Parapsychology has always existed on the fringes of the academic world, but rarely has it been tackled by anyone so unqualified. Their work wasn't peer-reviewed because they didn't have peers. They were all of twenty-two when they wrote it, with nothing more than undergrad degrees from a Big Ten school. *Ghosts from Our Past* was either the worst kind of hokum or an elaborate in-joke. For their benefit, I hoped for the latter.

Blessedly, I soon forgot all about the book. I guess a great number of other readers did too, because I couldn't find a used bookstore in the entire city that would take it off my hands. Their shelves were already stocked with unwanted copies, several of which were signed by Dr. Yates to coworkers at the Kenneth P. Higgins Institute of Science. One copy was personalized, *To Mom. Thanks for everything!*

My heart broke in two—for that poor mother. Can you imagine pouring eighteen years into raising a child, only to have her waste her life on spooks and specters?

The next time I heard their names, Yates and Gilbert were operating as paranormal exterminators under the name "Ghostbusters." The press covered their little undead dog-and-pony show as if they were reality TV stars running for president. The public ate it up. Suddenly, everyone in town was talking about ghosts, including colleagues of mine I'd previously respected. Either ghosts were real, or New Yorkers were collectively losing their minds.

Group delusions take many forms. One seventeenth-century afternoon in a French convent, a nun began meowing like a cat. Other nuns soon joined in, unable to help themselves. The meowing grew so loud that neighbors called the police, who arrived with nightsticks drawn. The threat of physical violence was apparently enough to return the nuns to their senses. They could not, for the life of them, recall why they'd started meowing in the first place.

Unfortunately, not all group delusions are as benign as those habit-wearing cat ladies. When a delusion is driven by fear—a belief in malevolent spirits threatening the Big Apple, for instance—sociologists use a different term to describe it: mass hysteria.

Thankfully, the group delusion that had taken hold of my fellow New Yorkers hadn't progressed that far . . . yet. Since no one else seemed up to the task of busting the Ghostbusters, I valiantly nominated myself. I didn't need a PKE meter or any other pseudoscientific gadgets to discredit them. I had the most advanced tool ever created on my side: the human brain. That, and a video camera. If you expose a fraud and don't document it on video, all you've done is expose yourself as an amateur.

Alas, ghosts are more than delusions. Spectral entities are real—and dangerous, which I learned in the most excruciatingly painful way possible. If only I'd taken Drs. Gilbert and Yates's research seriously, I could have saved myself thousands of dollars in out-of-pocket medical expenses.

Life is too short to be skeptical when it comes to spirits of the dead. Don't let the many months I spent in physical rehab be in vain. Please read this important book. My former colleagues at the CLD may laugh at me now, but you will thank me when paranormal activity personally plagues you.

—Martin Heiss, *former chairman of the Council for Logic and Data*

Introduction to the Revised Edition

BACK WHEN WE WROTE THE FIRST EDITION OF GHOSTS FROM OUR PAST, WE were young and green and full of Chinese takeout. We'd just graduated with bachelors of science in physics. One of us—Abby—planned to return to Michigan for grad school while the other—Erin—had been accepted into the physics program at Princeton. Our final summer together in Ann Arbor loomed before us. While the rest of our friends backpacked through Europe or attended Lilith Fair, we decided to write a book about ghosts.

It would be more than just a trial run for our eventual theses. We wanted to write a study so pioneering it would render every existing book on the paranormal obsolete.

Like many books surveying the supernatural, we planned to delve into the long cultural history of ghosts. Unlike most of those books, however, we would dive deep into the science behind spectral entities. Not pseudoscience. *Real* science. While we were all of twenty-two, the great thing about science is that it has no age requirement, so long as the work holds up. Our schooling was far from complete, but we knew just enough to be dangerous.

The ignorance of youth may have even worked in our favor: Our minds were unrestricted by the narrow hallways of academia. Much of the paranormal activity we examined had never been taken seriously by scientists before; most had never been taken seriously by *anyone* before.

Although we couldn't perform any experiments ourselves due to our non-existent budget and lack of lab space, we had a wealth of research papers, journals, and rare books at the U of M's Special Collections Library at our disposal. The undergraduate library next door was open twenty-four hours a day, meaning we could work around the clock. And our favorite Chinese place, Tomorrow's Teriyaki, graciously supported us in our endeavor by delivering directly to our temporary workspace.

Two weeks after sitting down, we had a single-spaced, 460-page manuscript that we christened *Ghosts from Our Past: Both Literally and Figuratively: The Study of the Paranormal*. Except for the autobiographical chapters, it was a genuine collaboration: We passed the laptop back and forth every other page, and sometimes every other sentence. Not to spoil anything, but our exhaustive research—combined with Erin's mindblowing firsthand experience with the paranormal—led us to the unassailable conclusion that GHOSTS ARE REAL.

We printed a truckload of copies but no one wanted them. We were too far ahead of our time. A promotional appearance on a campus talk show, *Wolverine Scene*, didn't play out the way we'd intended, and our friendship and the book both died quiet deaths.

Or so we thought. Years later, Abby discovered a copy propping up the monitor at her office, where it had apparently been sitting for fifteen-plus years. As she thumbed through it, a few things were painfully evident. We had gotten some stuff glaringly wrong, such as the squared x in the Yates-Gilbert Equation, which clearly should have been cubed. There's also one too many mentions of *The X-Files*—but, hey, it was the nineties. Our unbridled enthusiasm for seeking the truth about unexplained phenomena couldn't be untangled from our love of the show any more than you could untangle Mulder from Scully.

Overall, though, the book wasn't bad. Abby dug out the rest of our initial print run from storage and posted the books for sale online. Erin found this a little irritating. Not only was she not consulted, but Abby's actions almost brought about the Fourth Cataclysm. But we're all good now. These things happen. The important thing is that we're closer than ever. Near-death experiences are best when they're shared amongst friends!

The previous edition of *Ghosts from Our Past* has since been pulled in favor of the one you're reading now. We've updated it with the help of an editor, who suggested that we "organize" it into three parts: Our Stories (to share our backgrounds), Our Research (to present our findings), and Our Methods (to explain our process, so that others might follow our lead).

Outside of the final chapter, however, we haven't touched much of the original text—leave the past alone, we say. No need to go full George Lucas.

We've also left our original hand-drawn illustrations intact. It was either that or let those sophomore-year Studio: Drawing I classes go completely to waste.

Notably missing from this edition, however, are over two hundred pages of ghostly "orb" photographs taken in the depths of the rare-book room. Our pictures showed floating, glowing white spheres that had been invisible to the naked eye when we'd snapped them. *Finally*, we thought, *evidence of ghosts!* While the building may indeed be haunted, the mysterious orbs turned out to be nothing more than dust particles on Erin's camera lens.

There's plenty of fresh material for you to chew on, however, including a new foreword by an actual ghost and a buttload of new resources tacked on as an appendix. Our fellow Ghostbusters, Dr. Jillian Holtzmann and Patty Tolan, contributed new sections focusing on their respective areas of expertise. Our multitalented receptionist, Kevin, even wrote . . . a thing. Nice job, Kevin.

What hasn't changed is the way we're treated by the scientific community. Pioneers always suffer for their innovations—just look at what happened to trailblazers like Galileo Galilei and Archibald Dutton. Some people just won't be convinced that ghosts are real until one bites them on the gluteus maximus. As Jason Hawes, founder of the Atlantic Paranormal Society, says, "All a skeptic is is someone who hasn't had an experience yet."

To put it another way: Haters gonna hate, until they ain't.

We doubt you're a hater, though. You've made it this far. Since we're all friends here, we feel safe telling you this: It's okay if you're on the fence about this whole ghost business. We don't blame you for your caution; in fact, we applaud you. The great Carl Sagan said that extraordinary claims require extraordinary evidence. Who are we to argue with him (or his ghost)? We are unquestionably proposing some extraordinary concepts here. At the same time, it's one frigging extraordinary book.

Before you turn the page and dig into the evidence, we want you to pick up your phone. Do it. We're serious. Unless you're driving and listening to the audiobook. Or reading this on your phone, in which case you already have your phone in hand.

Got it? Good. Now we want you to call someone. Don't call the Ghostbusters—Kevin has enough to deal with as it is. The recent events in Manhattan have us swamped. Instead, call in sick to work tomorrow, because once you start reading *Ghosts from Our Past: Both Literally and Figuratively: The Study of the Paranormal,* you're not going to be able to stop.

In fact, you might not ever go back to work, because there's a good chance you'll want to strap on a proton pack and follow in our footsteps. To which we say, good luck! Just don't follow too closely—Erin has an itchy trigger finger.

—Erin Gilbert, Ph.D., M.S., and Abby L. Yates, Ph.D.

PART 1

Our Stories

PART 1—AT A GLANCE

TOO OFTEN, SCIENTISTS ARE ASSUMED TO BE NOTHING MORE than detached observers, teeming with an objectivity that separates us from the rest of humanity.

There is, however, a fire within every scientist.

We're not talking about heartburn, although a disproportionate number of scientists do suffer from indigestion. We're talking about the passion that burns within. Far from being detached observers, scientists are, at our core, passionate beings. You haven't witnessed real passion until you've visited an arboretum with a dendrologist. Hint: There's a lot of crying involved. Dendrologists tend to cry a lot, in fact. You'd cry too, if you spent that much time hanging out with trees.

How did we come to our passion for the paranormal? In the interest of full disclosure, we'll share our personal experiences with you in this section. In **Chapter 1**, you'll learn all about eight-year-old Erin's encounter with the Class IV next door. In **Chapter 2**, Abby shares the story of her childhood obsession with science, as well as the fateful meeting with Erin that spurred a lifelong friendship and intellectual rivalry. And finally, in **Chapter 3**, we will recount our shared experience as paranormal investigators and researchers in high school and college, as part of the Metaphysical Examination Society (of which we were the only two members).

Through our stories, we hope you will understand who we are, why we're fascinated by the paranormal, and why we've undertaken this important study.

CHAPTER 1

Ghost Girl:
That One Time I Saw a
Ghost (For Real)

Erin's Story

"DO YOU BELIEVE IN GHOSTS?"

It's a question I hear all the time. Frankly, I'm getting tired of it. As a scientist—physicist-in-training by day, paranormal investigator by night—it's more than a little insulting. Nobody asks Stephen Hawking if he believes in black holes. So why do people think it's okay to ask someone with a professed interest in the paranormal if they believe in ghosts?

Not only do I believe in them, but I saw one when I was eight.

Back when I was in elementary school, my family lived in a small suburban enclave in Battle Creek, Michigan. Does the name sound familiar? It should: Battle Creek is Cereal City, USA. Its name is printed on over half of all cereal boxes sold in the United States. Depending on which way the wind was blowing, our neighborhood would smell like either Apple Jacks or Fruity Pebbles.

Not everyone was a fan of the sugary smells permeating the city. Among the chief critics was a mean old lady who lived right next door, who could be heard ranting and raving about the air quality even on the clearest of days.

Now, to a kid, every adult is "old." I remember thinking my parents were ancient, even though they were only a couple of years older than I am right now. The woman next door, however, was old by anyone's standard. Her thin, white hair sprouted in sparse patches, like a poorly seeded Chia Pet.

Her wrinkled skin had more spots than a Dalmatian. In fact, she looked so much like the villain from *101 Dalmatians* that the neighbor kids had taken to calling her "Cruella." I'm ashamed to say I joined in. I had no other choice—nobody seemed to know her name, not even my parents . . . at least not until we read the obituary.

But I'm getting ahead of myself. Let me start from the beginning.

Devil's Night

My story starts late one October day in 1985—the day before Halloween, to be exact. In Detroit, the evening before All Hallow's Eve was known as Devil's Night. It was a night of vandalism for the sake of running wild. At least that was the story. In our little corner of suburbia, far from Motor City's dangerous streets, October 30 was just a fall night like any other. After school, my parents asked me to rake the backyard with Jimmy and Kate.

The twins were a couple of grades above me. Whenever there was yard work to do at the Gilberts, Jimmy and Kate would show up, gloves in hand. I labored under the delusion for years that they were my besties, before discovering that my parents were paying them a dollar an hour—not only to help out with chores but to be my friends.

I hadn't yet wised up to my parents' scam in 1985, so the three of us BFFs were busy raking the leaves into piles and then jumping in. The leaves would scatter, and we'd re-rake them and start all over again. Give a child a rake, and they'll never be bored. Or maybe that was just me, seeing as how my friends were paid to have "fun." Either way, we were making too much noise for Cruella, whose back door banged open.

The old woman flew onto the porch with supernatural speed. I gripped my wooden rake handle tightly. The rake was taller than I was, and it felt like I was clutching onto a sturdy tree to prevent being blown away. None of us dared say anything, even under our breath. Cruella's hearing, unlike my grandparents', was undiminished by age. Her eyesight was sharp as a hawk. The only sense affected by age appeared to be her sense of humor.

She cleared her throat, which sounded like someone trying to start a lawnmower. "If a single leaf ends up on my side of the property line, there will be hell to pay," she hissed. "Hell. To. Pay."

After she had disappeared back inside, the three of us did the most thorough job of raking and bagging leaves that anyone in southern Michigan had ever seen. Thank God it wasn't windy—who knows what would have happened if the wind had blown our leaves across Cruella's backyard, which was as barren as a postapocalyptic wasteland.

We hauled the bags to the curb, where the trash men would pick them up at the end of the week. The twins took off, and I hurried inside.

All Hallow's Eve

Every Halloween, I dressed up as the same thing: a ghost (Figure 1.1). When I was five, my mother cut a couple of eye holes in a white sheet and tossed it over me. The sheet was fitted for a king-size bed and trailed behind me on the ground like a bride's train. It was stained with dirt and grass, like . . . well, like it had been dragged around the neighborhood. My parents never washed the sheet between Halloweens—either they forgot, or just figured it wasn't worth the Tide.

While my costume didn't change the year in question, something did:

FIGURE 1.1.
Erin Gilbert, age 8.

I got to trick-or-treat without an adult chaperone for the first time. The twins, dressed as a witch and a werewolf, offered to take me around, giving my dad the night off.

We hit up about forty homes before the porch lights started going out. With the temperature dropping by the minute, I asked Jimmy and Kate if they wanted to call it a night. They shook their heads, and we marched on. Soon, practically every house had gone dark. It seemed pointless to continue trick-or-treating. If only I'd known then the real reason we were out so late: It was a holiday, so my "friends" were getting paid time and a half ($1.50 an hour) to escort me around.

We finally returned to our street sometime after ten o'clock. As we neared my driveway, Jimmy hoisted up one of the bags of leaves from the previous night. He turned toward Cruella's house. His eyes, just visible through his werewolf mask, glinted with mischief in the moonlight.

"Oh, no," I said from underneath my off-white sheet. "I'm not doing this."

"That's right," Kate said, picking up another bag. "You're not doing this—*we* are. That mean old witch deserves it."

It was a funny thing to hear come out of a pretend witch's mouth, but I let the incongruity slide. Cruella could have been a real witch, for all anybody knew. Not that there was anything wrong with that: My parents taught me to respect others' beliefs.

I pleaded with the twins to let it go, but they wanted retribution for her barking at us.

"She doesn't want a single leaf in her yard? She won't get a single leaf— she'll get hundreds of them," Jimmy announced, marching across the lawn to Cruella's darkened porch. I'd never seen the porch light turned on—not on Halloween, not ever. Cruella seemed to live in darkness.

Jimmy and Kate ripped open the bags and dumped the leaves on her doorstep. All I could do was stand there on the sidewalk, waving my arms in protest like an invisible, powerless specter.

Suddenly the door rattled open, sending the twins scattering in opposite directions. I didn't know who to follow. The only thing I knew was that I didn't want to run home, because then Cruella would know exactly who I was under my sheet.

Cruella busted out onto the porch. She pointed a bony index finger straight at me, singling me out from my fleeing friends. The wind picked up, sending the leaves at her feet into the air. They seemed to swirl around her, as if driven by unseen forces. Mentally, I prepared for the worst. Just because Cruella had never shot lightning bolts from her fingers before didn't mean it couldn't happen.

The porch light at my house clicked on. My mother stepped outside and saw me standing in front of Cruella's house. She followed my eyes to Cruella's porch, which was now empty. The old woman had apparently gone back inside.

I stared at her closed front door. Had I imagined the whole thing? No, my friends had been spooked too. One of their pumpkin baskets was over-turned in the bushes at the edge of our yard. Candy lay dumped in the grass. Any other time, I would have scrambled to pick it up—any other time but right now. All I wanted to do was get home, and get under the covers of my bed where I would be safe. I prayed the blinds on my window would be enough of a barrier between us. Little did I know, even the greatest of bar-riers could not prevent Cruella from getting her revenge.

The Death and Afterlife of Gretta DeMille

Days before Christmas, I heard a bunch of commotion next door. I cau-tiously opened my blinds for the first time since October to see a dozen neighbors on Cruella's front lawn. An ambulance and fire truck were parked in the street. The old woman must have been sick. I waited for her to be stretchered away, like the old man down the street who'd had a heart attack the previous year and gone to the hospital.

There would be no stretcher. After a couple of hours, two men carried a black body bag out through the snow and dumped it unceremoniously into the back of a hearse. Sad to say, but I felt an enormous sense of relief—not that somebody had died, but that the old woman would never frighten me again.

As we all later learned, Cruella—real name: Gretta DeMille—had bro-ken her hip in a fall a week or so earlier. She'd been lying there in the living room ever since, wasting away. In fact, the coroner believed she died the morning her body was discovered. Gretta was no witch. If she had been, she would have been able to heal herself or, at least, cast a spell to call for help. She was just a lonely woman with no real friends or family to speak of.

I don't remember what time I went to bed—probably around eight—but I remember what time I woke up: 2:06 in the morning. That was the time glowing red on my alarm clock when Gretta appeared at the foot of my bed.

The old woman was wearing her favorite house dress, a shapeless green-and-white-checkered sack that looked like a tablecloth. Except . . . some-thing was different. There was a faint phosphorescent glow around her, which seemed to indicate she wasn't of this world.

I was obviously having a nightmare. Still, that didn't make the sight any less terrifying. I tried to scream. Nothing came out of my mouth.

The apparition, however, wasn't so speechless. "Hell . . . to . . . pay, young girl," she whispered. "There will be . . . hell . . . to . . . pay . . ."

She began choking, as if she were trying to cough up a hairball.

It was no hairball.

Blood spilled out of her mouth, pouring down the front of her dress. It kept coming, too, cascading down her chin and neck like a crimson waterfall. She rose over the end of the bed, dripping blood onto the bedspread as her feet left the ground (Figure 1.2).

I pulled my covers over my head and shut my eyes tight. If I could only will myself awake, the nightmare would be over. Unfortunately, as the assault dragged on with no end in sight, I started to worry that I was already awake.

The sound of the blood pounding the sheet like rain on a tent kept me up until my alarm sounded for school, at which time it abruptly stopped. My ears popped, as if the air pressure had suddenly shifted. Cautiously, I lowered the sheet and peeked over the edge. The old woman was gone. So was the blood. The waking nightmare, or whatever it had been, was over.

Restless Nights and Anxious Days

I didn't say a word about my spectral encounter at the breakfast table. In the daylight, the whole event seemed outrageous. Ghosts weren't real. They were just silly things that kids dressed up as to go trick-or-treating.

However, as the sun set after dinner that night, the fear began to creep back in. Maybe Gretta's ghost had been more than a hallucination. Once I was tucked in and the lights were out, the corners of the room seemed to come alive. My heart rate spiked as the shadows danced. It was all in my mind, but even the most rational amongst us can be spooked in the dark. Our senses are easily tricked.

I switched the bedside lamp on. Immediately, the shadows disappeared. I'd been freaking myself out about nothing. I turned the lamp off and closed my eyes. After a while, I fell asleep.

Six minutes after two, my slumber was shattered once again. The ghost was at the foot of my bed. Before she could start spitting blood, though, I turned on the bedside lamp. It had worked to dispel the shadows . . .

. . . but it didn't work to dispel Gretta.

She grinned at me, showing off a mouthful of empty sockets. The terror struck me even harder than the previous night. There could be no question

FIGURE 1.2.
This is how I remember Gretta's ghost. The image still terrifies me, even today.

about it: This was no dream. As she rose up off the floor and repeated her routine from the previous evening, I threw the covers over my head.

I may have eventually made it back to sleep that second night—frankly, I don't remember. Because it wasn't the last time the spook terrorized me. Gretta appeared in my room in the early morning hours every single night . . . FOR THE NEXT YEAR. So it wasn't just technically one time that I saw a ghost—it was hundreds of times.

You're probably wondering why I didn't just tell my parents about the ghost in my bedroom. Here's the thing: *I did tell them.* The morning after the

Scared to Death!

While ghosts are often described as being "transparent," most are not as intangible as they might seem. As you'll learn in later chapters, paranormal entities are capable of interacting physically with our world and wreaking havoc. Even when incorporeal, they have been known to literally scare people to death. (It totally happens!) The many dangers of ghosts include:

- Property damage
- Emotional trauma, classified in the *Diagnostic and Statistical Manual of Mental Disorders-IV* as PPSD (Post-Paranormal Stress Disorder)
- Cardiac arrest, caused by extreme fright
- Physical injury, up to and including death

second incident. They were skeptical, but agreed to take turns camped out in my bedroom that night. Of course, Gretta never showed up with them in the room—but when they left or fell asleep, she would reappear, with a smile even more fiendish than before.

My parents put me in therapy for my paranormal "problem." Once a week, a therapist named Dick Rockwell asked me about my life. He asked about my parents, about school, and about my ghost. Whenever I brought up Gretta, he simply nodded, and said, "That's very interesting. Why do you think she does this?" To which I replied, *Isn't that a question you should be asking her? She's the one that should be in therapy, not me!*

Even though studies have repeatedly shown widespread belief in spooks and specters, few are willing to publicly admit their beliefs. I was no different. I didn't mention the old woman's ghost to anyone but my parents and Dick Rockwell, but word still got out. My parents must have talked to their friends about it at some dinner party, and then they told their kids. It took me a couple of weeks to catch on that everyone at school knew. Once I figured that out, though, all the kids yelling "Boo!" at me made a lot more sense.

My paranormal experience confirmed for my classmates what they'd always believed: I was strange. I was obsessed with getting straight A's, even in kindergarten when we weren't assigned letter grades. And while everyone else was struggling to make it through Dr. Seuss, I was inching my way through Carl Sagan's *Cosmos*. I was used to being called "Nerd." After the ghost story circulated, I picked up an even more hurtful name: "Ghost Girl."

That may sound innocuous. For an eight-year-old already struggling with nightly spectral visits, however, it nearly broke me. After about a year, Gretta stopped visiting me. Had she gotten bored of frightening me, or simply lost the power to materialize in our world?

Either way, I felt the effects of those nightly scare sessions for much longer. Every time someone called me Ghost Girl, I was reminded of the restless nights I'd endured. My anxiety spiked. Today, doctors would call it PPSD. Back then, my therapist just told me to "get over it."

I often wonder if Gretta's ghost ever visited the twins. Unfortunately, they stopped being my friends—for any price. If anyone would have believed me, I thought it would have been them. There was only one person who ever believed me, and I would have to wait until the eleventh grade to meet her . . . but when we did meet, she would push me to overcome my fear of ghosts by confronting it head-on. No more hiding under the sheets.

And with that, I'll turn you over to her. Here's Abby!

CHAPTER 2

Curious Georgina: Portrait of a Young Supernatural Scientist
Abby's Story

RIOR TO THE TWENTIETH CENTURY, THE MOST IM-portant trait for a young scientist to have was a set of male genitalia. Thankfully, physicist Marie Curie changed that by winning the Nobel Prize in 1903, and these days, curiosity is the most important trait for a young scientist.

After all, science is nothing if not a series of questions: How do birds fly? What causes lightning? Are pirate ghosts the ghosts of pirates, or are they ghosts that became pirates in the afterlife?

Since you already know I'm a world-class scientist, it should come as no surprise that I was an exceptionally curious child.

Going Bananas

I've always loved asking questions—about anything and everything. My first word wasn't "Mama," "Dada," or "Higgs boson." My first word was "Why"—followed quickly by "What this?" And then I said "Higgs boson."

They are the eternal questions of childhood. Yet they have driven parents nuts for centuries, mostly because adults often don't know the answers themselves. Even the simplest question may have a complex answer. A child picks up a rock and asks her mother, "What this?" It's virtually the same question the first Neanderthal scientist asked when picking up a rock. Neanderthals never learned the answer to that question, but tens of thousands of years later modern humans learned rocks are made of minerals. Centuries after that, scientists discovered those minerals are made of atoms. And decades after that discovery, physicists discovered even smaller particles called quarks and leptons. That's a pretty deep dive, so most parents will just cut their kids off and say it's a damn rock.

If I picked up a rock, I had to know what it was made of, where it came from, and why it tasted funny when I licked it. Because of my intense curiosity, my parents called me "Curious Georgina." A cute nickname when you're a toddler, but embarrassing when the other kids overhear your mother calling you their "little monkey" at the third grade science fair.

The day after the fair, a group of half a dozen girls cornered me on the playground. They looked like trouble. Kacey Lambertson pulled an enormous bunch of bananas out of a paper bag and held them out to me. "Hungry?" she said with a smirk.

When faced with danger, our fight-or-flight response is supposed to kick in. Mine must have been broken. Instead of throwing a fist or running off, I snatched the bananas out of her hand and proceeded to eat them. Down the hatch they went, one after the other, until all that was left were thirteen empty peels and a gurgling stomach.

"Thanks," I said. "That really hit the spot."

The girls were speechless.

An hour later during a math lesson, I blacked out.

I woke up in an intensive care unit. An IV drip was hooked up to my arm. Apparently, potassium poisoning is a thing! It's called "hyperkalemia," and can lead to renal failure and cardiac arrest if not immediately treated. Science!

Hunting the Elusive *Leipreachán*

Despite my brush with mortality, I couldn't help my natural curiosity. And so, a few weeks later, I set off on an ill-fated quest to reach the end of a rainbow.

I'd heard about leprechauns and their pots of gold at the ends of rainbows, of course. Most of my education on the legendary Irish fairies had come to me by way of Lucky Charms. To say the least, I was extremely skeptical of the claims made by General Mills. The frosted marshmallows were certainly delicious, but were they *magically* delicious? There was only one

FIGURE 2.1.
Zorp, Abby's Imaginary Dog

way to find out: Follow the rainbow to the very end and see if leprechauns were real.

(Yeah, I know what you're thinking: *Leprechauns? Isn't this book supposed to be about ghosts?* Well, not all of us could be as lucky as Erin and see a ghost when we were kids. Even if it did terrify the living neutrons out of her. So hang with me here.)

One day, following a big thunderstorm, I was playing in the backyard with my imaginary dachshund, Zorp (Figure 2.1). (Yes, he was named after the Class VII metaspecter.) Before you go off thinking I had lost my mind, let me state that my mother was allergic to dogs. An imaginary one was the only kind I was allowed to have.

I looked up and saw a massive rainbow, shimmering in the late afternoon sky like half a McDonald's arch. It couldn't have been more than a hundred yards away. I'd gone further into the woods and found my way out before—I harbored dreams of being an explorer of unknown worlds like Sally Ride, the first American female astronaut. While my parents didn't have the money to send me to space camp, they let me have free range in the woods. We lived in Rochester, a small town on the outskirts of Detroit. Bad stuff was always happening in the big city. Nothing bad ever happened out in Rochester. Except for wolverine attacks.

I tore off through the woods in the direction of the rainbow. No matter how fast my legs carried me, however, it didn't get any closer. Deeper and deeper I went, farther than I'd ever gone.

After ten minutes or so, the rainbow faded. My shoulders slumped in defeat. I turned around and started trudging back the way I'd come.

Except that I found myself in uncharted territory—there were no landmarks to help me chart my course back home. After an hour of wandering aimlessly, I gave up. I was lost. With horror, I realized I wasn't going to be the next Sally Ride; I was going to be the next Amelia Earhart. Zorp was no help. His allergies were acting up, and he couldn't sniff his way back. I'd have to take him to an imaginary vet and get him some imaginary antihistamines. But we had to get home first.

My father once told me that if I ever got lost, to sit still and let someone find me. "If you go wandering around while someone else is searching for you," he said, "you'll just lead everyone in circles. And then you're not missing—you're leading a parade through the woods. That's pretty neat if all the deer and squirrels join up, but less cool if the wolverines do and they start attacking everyone."

For three days and two nights, Zorp and I huddled beneath a large maple tree, which protected us from the elements. We survived by drinking fresh rainwater off leaves and eating imaginary dog food. It was no Lucky Charms, but it was better than Cheerios.

If you don't remember my dimples all over the news, that's probably because my face wasn't shown on TV when I went missing. There was no

FIGURE 2.2.
Leprechauns: Real or Fake?

search party, no benefit concert to find Abby L. Yates. My father simply
showed up on the third day around supper time and asked me if I was ever
coming home.

My parents had known where I was the whole time. My father had found
me sleeping under the tree and left dinner out for me, which the wolverines
must have eaten. He'd also brought dry dog food for Zorp. So I wasn't eating
imaginary dog food after all! Ha ha. Ugh. Let's just keep that detail between
you and me.

I wasn't angry with my parents, even though being left alone that long in
the woods did sting a little. (The stinging turned out to be the poison oak I'd
been using for toilet paper. I recovered, though, and now you can barely see
the scars!) Still, I'm thankful my parents indulged my every whim. Even if

sometimes they couldn't tell the difference between me playing around and me fearing for my life in the woods.

While I never did find out if leprechauns were real—the jury is still out (Figure 2.2)—I *did* eventually find out what made Lucky Charms so magically delicious: sugar. Three teaspoons per serving. Just one of the many exciting facts I learned at the Dry Breakfast Foods Museum in Battle Creek, Michigan, which my family visited on vacation the next year. Little did any of us know that just a few short years later we would be living in Cereal City, USA—and that I would meet a kindred scientific spirit by the name of Erin Gilbert.

First Contact

I called my mother Mom, but to most people she was Dr. Cynthia Yates, the first woman to earn a doctorate in chemical physics from Iowa State University.

The 1950s weren't a good time for women in science. My mother kept her head down and forged a career nonetheless, first as a researcher at Tulane University and later in the private sector, as head of chemical engineering at Schorning Chemical. If you don't recognize the company's name, you surely know the jingle from Schorning's commercials, which aired endlessly during Saturday morning cartoons (*We make the chemicals / That make up your plastic toys / Found in four of five cereals / Safe for both girls and boys*). As it turns out, one of those chemicals—hydrazine polycarbonate—wasn't safe for girls or boys. It was an endocrine-disrupting compound, which caused the early onset of puberty in millions of children in the seventies and early eighties.

My mother was the first to discover the dangers of hydrazine polycarbonate. When her bosses told her to keep quiet about it, she took it to the FDA. Unfortunately, there were no whistle-blower protections at the time. She was fired—a major blow, since she was the breadwinner in our family. Thankfully, she found a new job in Battle Creek, where she could put her skills as a biochemist to work fortifying cereals with essential vitamins and minerals.

I was already a month into the first semester of my junior year. I begged and pleaded with my parents to leave me behind with my aunt and uncle to finish out high school. There weren't even any woods in Battle Creek.

They'd cut down all the trees to make room for cereal factories! Plus, I dreaded having to make new friends.

They reminded me that I didn't have any friends at my old school.

So I lost that fight and packed my boxes. My uncle gave me some tips on adjusting to a new environment. Specifically, to avoid being bullied by other girls, I should walk up to the baddest-looking girl on the first day and casually slip a shank into her side. Perhaps it's a good thing I didn't stay behind with them.

What I did do on my first day of school was keep to myself. So, not a big change from my old routine. Nobody approached me, even to bully me, which I found a little insulting. I'd been expecting some minor hazing, like what happens to the new kid in teenage movies. Maybe some girl would slap a Post-it Note on my back reading KICK ME. Or maybe some insecure guy would knock my lunch tray out of my hands. But apparently nobody pranked the new kid anymore, at least not at Hoover High. They were too busy picking on existing students to worry about me.

I quickly identified their chief target: a beanpole dressed like a librarian. The other kids called her "Ghost Girl," which was about the awesomest nickname I'd ever heard. (Better than Curious Georgina, at least.) We were the only two kids in Chemistry who ever bothered to raise our hands. At lunch, we both sat by ourselves, which was particularly insulting, since there weren't enough tables for *anyone* to be eating by themselves; a couple of girls chose to eat standing up against the brick wall rather than sit with either of us. After a week of this ridiculousness I went straight from the lunch line to Ghost Girl's table.

"Is this seat taken?" I asked, nodding toward an empty seat across from her.

She looked up at me, startled as if she were a deer caught in headlights. It wouldn't have surprised me if she had scampered off on all fours like a deer.

"Real funny," she said. "Like I haven't heard that one before. There's not a ghost in the chair, if that's what you're asking. You can move along now."

I contemplated moving along, but Mama didn't raise no quitter. I sat down. "Anyone who asks if there's a ghost in this chair doesn't know a damn thing about ghosts," I said. "Ghosts might have supernatural origins, but they're composed of ectoplasm, which appears on the visible light spectrum. If there were a ghost here, we'd both be able to see it."

"That's comforting," she said.

We sat in silence for a minute, and then I spoke up. "You . . . didn't see a ghost sitting here, did you?"

"God, no. You see one stupid ghost, and suddenly everyone thinks you're some sort of ghost whisperer."

"Okay, because if you did, you can tell me," I said. "I'm Abby, by the way."

"Erin," she muttered.

"So it's true? You've seen a ghost?"

Erin glanced around the cafeteria nervously. "You're not going to make fun of me, are you? Because if you are—"

"I wouldn't do that," I said, crossing myself. "Girl Scout's honor." I'd never been in the Scouts, but I respected what they did.

She inhaled and exhaled loudly, as if she were about to go into labor. She leaned across the table. "When I was eight . . . I saw the ghost of an old woman who lived next door."

"Was she dead?"

"Of course she was dead! How could I see her ghost if she wasn't dead?"

I shrugged. "Could be an astral projection."

"An astral *what?*"

"Astral projection. It's when your astral body leaves your physical body, sort of like how the soul departs your body upon death. I don't necessarily believe in it, but it's one possibility."

Erin contemplated this. "What other possibilities are there?"

"That you hallucinated the whole thing. Did anyone else see the ghost?" She shook her head.

"Then that's another possibility," I said. "But I believe *you* believe you saw a ghost. I mean, you wouldn't call yourself Ghost Girl for nothing."

"Someone else started calling me that."

"Kids can be cruel," I said, nodding.

"My second-grade teacher came up with the name."

"Ouch."

"You're telling me." Erin paused and smiled for the first time. "You know, you're the first person who I've talked to about ghosts in years who hasn't called me crazy."

"Oh, you could still be crazy," I said, "but that doesn't preclude you from seeing ghosts. Crazy people see ghosts just the same as everybody else. For what it's worth, you don't seem crazy. You seem kind of . . . cool."

Suddenly her smile fell. "How much are my parents paying you?"

When I expressed ignorance, she explained how her parents had paid a couple of neighbor kids a buck an hour to be her friend when she was younger. It was the saddest thing I'd ever heard. Right then and there I offered to be her friend . . . at the bargain rate of seventy-five cents an hour.

Erin accepted, and we've been the best of friends ever since. By now she probably owes me about $13,679.50, if my calculations are correct (and they're always correct, except when they're not). But I'd never ask her to pay up. For one thing, we're both so far in debt with student loans there's no way she's ever going to have that kind of money just sitting around. Also, I should be the one paying her for her friendship. Nobody else would have had the figurative balls to join me in founding the Metaphysical Examination Society, Hoover High's first-ever paranormal investigations club.

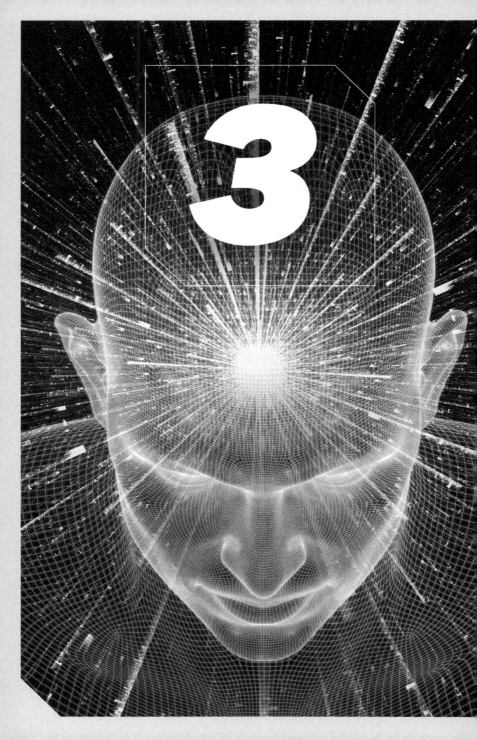

CHAPTER 3

The Metaphysical Examination Society
Our Story

T IS HUMAN NATURE TO FEAR THE UNKNOWN. THERE IS NO greater unknown than what awaits us after we take our final breath. It is life's great unanswered question.

If the fear of the unknown comes to us naturally, however, so too does the fear of those who take interest in it. Those who have sought out explanations for the afterlife outside the hallowed walls of religion have long been branded as heretics.

Nobody explicitly called us "heretics," of course, because nobody at Hoover High had any idea what that word meant. They just knew we were into spooky things. Our unnatural obsession with the paranormal was a bit like somebody who leaves their Halloween decorations up year round: Acceptable for the month of October, but mildly disturbing the rest of the year.

Perhaps we shouldn't have written and performed a musical based on *The Shining* for the school talent show. We'll also allow that our interpretation of "School Spirit Week" was wildly off-base—nobody wants to see spectral effigies torched during the homecoming parade. We get that now. Whatever the reasons, though, we weren't just unpopular. We were shunned.

Not that we cared. While all of the other kids in high school were busy going to parties and playing lawn darts or whatever, we were all like, "That's stupid." That's what Erin would literally say every time we overheard some girl in class talking about a rad party. And we heard about some great ones at Hoover High—ragers with DJs, kegs, and bouncy houses. Okay, not that last part, but that would have been the only thing that made a party cool in our eyes. Nobody was interested in hearing our opinion, though. Perhaps picking up on the vibe that we weren't accepting invitations, nobody ever invited us.

Besides being social outcasts, we were extracurricular outcasts too. We weren't interested in any after-school activities, like sports (too many bruises), chess club (too many rigid rules), or marching band (too fascist). Fed up, we decided to form a club of our own.

Ghost Clubbin'

As long as there have been ghosts, there have been ghost hunters. Whatever you call them—paranormal investigators, conductors of metaphysical examinations, psychical researchers, or supernatural scientists—they have been out there in the field, doing the work that few others have judged worthy of their time and attention. Over the years, they have banded together to form organizations such as the Ghost Club and the Society for Psychical Research (which we'll talk about more in Chapter 5).

Unfortunately, there were no local branches of these illustrious groups in Battle Creek, Michigan, when we were in high school. We had no choice but to forge our own path. We called our club . . . THE METAPHYSICAL EXAMINATION SOCIETY (Figure 3.1).

We turned our table for two in the school cafeteria into our meeting space every lunch hour. Abby pushed Erin to explore the strange world of the supernatural—to confront, rather than run from, her fear of the ghost in her past. With Abby's help, Erin learned to embrace her nickname. For good measure, Abby adopted it herself. Two Ghost Girls are better than one!

We shared notes and discussed the latest paranormal research. We read everything about ghosts we could get our hands on from the public library, with the eventual goal being an on-site inspection of a real haunted house—a metaphysical examination, in paraterminology.

Sadly, we never set foot in a single haunted house while in high school. We didn't know the first thing about finding a location to investigate. Not that we had the kind of money we thought you needed to perform metaphysical examinations. We spent hours scouring electronics catalogs, marveling at EMF meters and Geiger counters far out of our price range.

FIGURE 3.1.
Metaphysical Examination Society Meeting Notes

Senior year, however, we finally got a chance to put our growing knowledge of the paranormal to good use. Our AP Physics teacher, Mr. Gannon, broke us off into groups of four. He assigned us topics for the science fair. We forget what topic our team was supposed to explore, but we took some creative liberties and switched it up to focus on the paranormal. Our partners, Robin and Ben, weren't too pleased with us taking such a wildly different direction. They bowed out of the project, which we performed at the fair as a rap (copied here from memory). Abby had a little experience with the rap genre already—she used to spit rhymes with this little blond neighbor kid when she would visit her aunt and uncle in Detroit. Marshall something. Great kid. A little tightly wound.

NUTHIN' BUT A GHOST THANG

Spoken Word Intro

Erin: Oh my God, Abby. Look at that ghost. It's so big. It looks like
one of those composite ghosts.
Abby: Whoa, you're blowin' people's minds, E. A composite *what*?
Erin: A composite ghost, which consists of multiple interconnected entities.
Abby: There's, like, seriously brain matter all over this room right now. Minds be
blowin' up for real. Who knew there were different types of ghosts?
Erin and Abby: (together) We knew!
Erin: Yo. How many different types of ghosts we got, A?

Verse (Abby)

Humanoids, vapors, several dozen more
Free-roaming, anchored, are you keeping score?
Possessing, repeating, alone or in swarms
Powerful metaspecters changing forms

Chorus (Erin)

Ain't nuthin' but a ghost thang, baby
We ain't talking 'bout no Patrick Swayze
Ghosts are real, there ain't no "maybe"
Why does everybody say we crazy?

Actually, let's cut it off right there.

Mr. Gannon told us we were making a mockery of science. And of rap.
It didn't matter. We were leaving for college in the fall. In Ann Arbor, we'd
meet forward-thinking professors who would embrace us for our unconven-
tional beliefs. Like people undergoing near-death experiences, we could see
the light at the end of the tunnel.

Ann Arbor Days

At the University of Michigan, we tested out of the lower-level lib-
eral arts courses. We went straight into the good stuff: Physics 107—
Twentieth-Century Concepts of Space, Time, and Matter; Physics
115—Principles of Physics; and Quantum Mechanics I.

The professors were every bit as open-minded as we'd anticipated . . . except when it came to the paranormal. They believed in higher dimensions,

but make even a tiny suggestion that interdimensional entities could cross over into our world and you'd be laughed out of the classroom. We know, because that's exactly what happened to us in Professor Rice's Quantum Mechanics I course. It was high school all over again.

Unsurprisingly, we never really connected with our new classmates. There was an unbridgeable gap, and it wasn't just our belief in the paranormal. We simply weren't into what the other kids were into (drinking, Wolverines football games, and drinking). Who needed friends when we had each other? Unfortunately, the heavy course load—plus our part-time jobs in the dorm cafeteria—meant the Metaphysical Examination Society took a backseat.

During our sophomore year, we signed up for the most advanced course available for undergrads: Professor Alderman's Particle Physics & Theoretical Cosmology. When we walked into his classroom on the first day, we were greeted by row after row of empty desks. We later learned we were the only students brave enough to sign up for the notoriously tough class.

"Glad you could make it," a bearded and bespectacled man said. He was about our parents' age, and spoke with a vaguely Eastern European accent. He was busy writing a complex equation out on the chalkboard, and didn't turn to face us. Such was our introduction to the infamous Professor Alderman.

Erin muttered a weak apology, and we took seats in the very back of the classroom. The overhead lights were turned off, the room lit only by what little light filtered through the blinds.

"You can sit closer—I'm not going to bite," the professor said. He turned to us as we moved up a row. "Do either of you have the text?"

We nodded and raised our books triumphantly. Professor Alderman snatched Abby's book away. He flipped through it with a sneer on his face. "Theoretical cosmology is evolving much too fast for print," he said. "This text was published last year, and half the theories are already out of date."

He strolled back to the front of the room, where he casually tossed the two-hundred-dollar book into the wastebasket. The professor was as eccentric as advertised. Still, he seemed to sweat knowledge from his pores as he launched into his first lesson. Or maybe that was just sweat.

Discovering the Truth

A couple of weeks passed. We were just beginning to get the hang of our fall schedules when our world was shattered. The exact date is forever etched into our memories:

Friday, September 10.

The day *The X-Files* premiered.

It was like somebody had drawn up a list of our favorite things and turned it into a TV show. The FBI's X-files—investigated by two incredibly photogenic agents—covered paranormal phenomena from unexplained flying objects to cryptids. Special Agent Dana Scully, played by Gillian Anderson, even had a bachelor of science in physics. She was a smart, successful woman kicking ass. That would have been enough right there to get us to tune in, week after week. But there was more. Much more.

There was Fox Mulder (Figure 3.2).

While Scully was the scientist, we saw more of ourselves in her partner, played with dry wit by David Duchovny. Mulder was a believer. "The truth is out there," he famously said. That's all any scientist wants: to discover the truth. He wasn't just obsessed with explaining the unexplainable—much like us, "Spooky" Mulder was consumed by it. He was a fellow weirdo.

Is there life on other planets? Maybe.

Does it visit Earth? Anything's possible.

Would David Duchovny ever return our fan mail? We wanted to believe.

A Fateful Turn of Events

A couple of days later, we were whispering about whether Mulder and Scully would ever hook up when Professor Alderman paused his lecture and called us out. "Is there something more important than electric quadrupole moments?" he asked with irritation in his voice.

Erin was too embarrassed to answer, but Abby jumped right in. "I don't know if it's more important," she said, "but it's pretty close. We were discussing *The X-Files*."

The professor narrowed his eyes. "I've heard of it. Aliens, right?"

"And other stuff," Abby said. "Cryptozoological creatures, the paranormal—"

FIGURE 3.2.
FBI Special Agent Fox Mulder

"The paranormal?" Professor Alderman said, setting his chalk down. "You don't . . . believe in that sort of stuff, do you?"

It sounded more like an accusation than a question. Abby started to answer, but Erin kicked her under the desk. Pointedly ignoring her, Abby responded to the professor: "We have an open mind about it. Unlike some people."

"This is a rather fateful turn of events," Professor Alderman said. "The rest of the physics department here—hell, the rest of the university—are goats. They don't believe in the paranormal." He paused to smile. "But I do."

"You're kidding," Erin said.

"I've never made a joke in my life," he said, "and I'm not about to start now."

We had to take him at his word. His teaching style was rather severe and mostly consisted of him mumbling to himself while scratching out equations on the chalkboard. He wasn't the joking type.

As he would go on to explain, he held dual degrees—one in physics, and one in parapsychology. He'd previously taught parapsychology at the New York Institute of Technology, making him one of the few supernatural researchers to ply his trade within an academic setting. Not only was he an educator, but he was a ghost hunter who had traveled the globe investigating haunted locales in his free time.

"If any of this gets out, I could be fired," he cautioned us. We swore to take his secret to the grave. Although now we're publishing it, so . . . sorry? But not sorry. Read on.

Our First Ghost Hunt (Finally!)

Since we were the only two students in Professor Alderman's course, talk often turned to the paranormal. He had some interesting theories about the way the paranormal intersected with particle physics. It would eventually become one unified field of study, he said. He seemed surprised at first that we could keep up with his ideas, but quickly caught on that we'd done plenty of our own research. We weren't just a couple of novice ghostheads. We were the real deal.

Our final exam was scheduled for December 18. When we arrived in the classroom, however, he told us the final had been moved to later in the evening. He instructed us to meet him in the campus parking lot that night. "Bring a couple of flashlights and as many batteries as you can find," he said. "And dress appropriately for the weather. We'll be going on a little field trip."

Michigan was in the grip of a bitter cold spell, so we bundled up in our best winter gear—ski goggles, stocking caps, and parkas so big they made us look like a couple of polar bears that ate other polar bears. We met Professor Alderman at ten o'clock. He was dressed as usual in his brown sports jacket with elbow patches, looking every bit the same as he did every Tuesday and Thursday afternoon. The below-freezing weather didn't seem to bother him.

He looked us up and down. "You girls ready to go on your first metaphysical examination?"

It was finally happening!!!!!!!

"Then let's go," he said, reading the looks on our faces. He slung a duffel bag over his shoulder and started toward the parking lot exit, on foot.

We arrived at an ordinary-looking ranch house about a mile off campus. We knew that paranormal activity could happen anywhere—it happened at Erin's house, after all, and nothing is quite so mundane as your own house—but we'd been hoping our first real field excursion would be something a little more traditional. You know, an old Victorian home lit up from within like a jack-o'-lantern, with a couple of gargoyles standing guard at the entryway for good measure.

We stopped behind Professor Alderman on the front porch. "Are you nervous?" Abby asked Erin. "You're not having, like, flashbacks . . ."

"No way," Erin said. She'd been scared of Gretta once upon a time, but that had been long ago. People change. They grow up. For instance, Erin hated broccoli when she was a kid. Now she only sort of dislikes it.

Professor Alderman shushed us. "Don't want to scare away the ghosts," he explained, turning the doorknob. The professor ushered us inside. The room was dark—not ominously so, but dark enough. He turned on a lamp on an end table, but left the overhead lights off.

As he pulled tools out of his duffel bag, he told us the story of the mysterious goings-on at the house. The phenomena commenced some months ago when the owner, a single woman, started to feel uneasy for no apparent reason. At first she thought it was just anxiety, but soon unexplained chills were creeping up and down her spine. She started seeing things out of the corner of her eye . . . dark, shapeless things. When the shower ran red with blood, she finally gave her old professor a call.

He handed us each an audiotape recorder. During the stakeout—which he estimated would last four or five hours—we would sit still in a room and hold the recorders as they ran, changing the tape as necessary. While he didn't expect us to hear anything, such devices have been known to pick up spectral voices heard only on playback—so-called "electronic voice phenomena," or EVP. The professor said he needed to hit the bathroom. With that, he disappeared down a dark hallway, leaving us alone in the living room.

After about fifteen minutes, Erin went to check the kitchen for something to eat. Standing around doing nothing can be pretty taxing work! Erin stared inside the fridge, as if gazing into the abyss. Nothing spooky, mind you. Just a lot of junk food. Erin sniffed at a carton of chocolate milk, which had apparently gone bad sometime in the Reagan era. She shut the fridge. When she turned around, she came face-to-face with a woman in a robe.

To Erin's credit, she didn't scream.

The woman, however, did.

She pointed at Erin. "GHOST!"

Erin swung her head around, searching frantically in the low light. "Where? I don't see anything."

"You're not a ghost?" the woman asked, catching her breath.

"We're college students," Abby said, joining them in the kitchen. "And if anyone's a ghost here, it's you."

The woman flipped on the overhead light. "If you're not ghosts, what are you doing in my house?"

"We're on a paranormal investigation," Erin said. "With Professor Alderman."

"Professor—" The woman caught herself, and then nodded. "You mean James. Was tonight the night of the stakeout? I told him I'd be staying with my sister. I'm so sorry." She paused. "Where is he?"

We explained that he'd left to use the bathroom down the hall, but we hadn't seen him in at least twenty minutes. "He must have a copy of *Scientific American*," Erin said. "Sometimes you just start reading, and, next thing you know, an hour's passed."

Abby glared at her roommate. "That explains so much—about you, that is. But maybe we should check on him. Make sure he wasn't attacked by a ghost or something."

The woman agreed, and disappeared down the hallway.

Seconds later, we heard her scream.

We rushed down the hall and found her standing at the open bathroom door. "What is it?" Abby asked, peering over the woman's shoulder. "Is there blood in the shower again?"

The woman stood mute, pointing at Professor Alderman. He was slumped back on the toilet with his jeans bunched around his ankles, a blank expression on his worn face. He wasn't breathing. At his feet lay a copy of *Scientific American*, which had slipped out of his dead hands.

The Journey Begins

An autopsy later confirmed our professor died of a heart attack. Frightened to death by something he saw in the bathroom of the woman's house, or from natural causes? We may never know for sure.

By the time we gave our statements to police, it was two in the morning. The homeowner (whose name we're withholding) gave us her condolences. She zipped up Professor Alderman's duffel bag of paratechnological gadgets and handed it to us. The professor, she explained, had no family. His students were his family—and we were his only students this semester. Ergo, we were the closest thing he had to a next of kin.

We slept until noon the next day. When we woke up, we rewound the recordings we'd made the previous night. Erin had shut her audio recorder off when she'd gone to the kitchen, but Abby had accidentally let hers run in the living room for the length of the tape—sixty full minutes. We didn't expect to hear much more than static and the sounds of our voices in the background, and we were right . . . up until the 52:43 mark. That's when a man's voice broke through: "THE TRUTH . . . IS OUT . . . THERE."

Every time we listened to the tape, the words seemed a little different. EVP is notoriously difficult to decipher. Was this Professor Alderman's voice, relaying a message to us from beyond the grave? Another specter that haunted the woman's house? A stray radio signal picked up by the tape? The truth was out there, and it was up to us—not the FBI—to find it.

We immediately quit our jobs in the cafeteria. Without our boring part-time jobs, we had plenty of time for the Metaphysical Examination Society. We took out additional student loans and donated plasma to cover our living expenses. We had Professor Alderman's bag of ghost-hunting equipment, which aided our transition from lunch ladies to ghost hunters. We would carry on his work. If he was out there somewhere, we would make him proud.

We even convinced some homeowners to let us into their houses to investigate, something we'd struggled for years to do. Whether it was our newfound confidence or simply that we presented ourselves as professionals, things had certainly changed. We spent thousands of hours outside our classes chasing ghosts—both literally and figuratively, to echo this book's subtitle.

We witnessed some strange, unexplainable phenomena over the past two and a half years while juggling the paranormal with our school work, but no confirmed spectral entities (Erin's childhood vision of Gretta DeMille notwithstanding). Professor Alderman never spoke to us again or showed himself. That might sound like we failed. Quite the contrary: We succeeded insofar as we honed our techniques through trial and error, to such a degree that we're now able to pass that knowledge on to you.

What follows in this book is everything we've picked up along the way on our journey as conductors of metaphysical examinations—and as best friends.

Our Research

PART 2–AT A GLANCE

ALTHOUGH WE ARE NOW ON THE CUSP OF THE TWENTY-first century, we can only identify 4 percent of the matter in the universe. What else could be out there besides planets and stars and the vacuum of space? According to astronomers, the missing 96 percent of the universe is actually DARK MATTER and DARK ENERGY.

No one knows what type of particles dark matter and dark energy are composed of, because scientists haven't gotten their hands on any. In fact, no one has even observed dark matter or dark energy through a telescope. Yet we believe it is out there because we have observed its effects on the rest of the universe.

Along those same lines, no one has ever dragged a ghost into a lab for testing. We believe ghosts exist, however, in part because we have witnessed their effects upon parapercipients throughout history. We've spent untold hours researching the paranormal, and we're going to unload it all on you in this section.

Chapter 4 is our attempt at an abbreviated cultural history of ghosts. In **Chapter 5**, we will look at the investigators who paved the way for our current understanding of the paranormal. In **Chapter 6**, we will examine the science behind the supernatural, which is at least twice as spooky as dark matter and dark energy. And in **Chapters 7 and 8**, we will survey the various attempts made to classify and categorize ghosts, including the now-standard Spectral Classification Table found in *Kemp's Spectral Field Guide*. If all of that doesn't split your mind open like an atom during nuclear fission, we will give you a full refund on the purchase price of this book.*

---

* *Offer expires 10/31/97.*

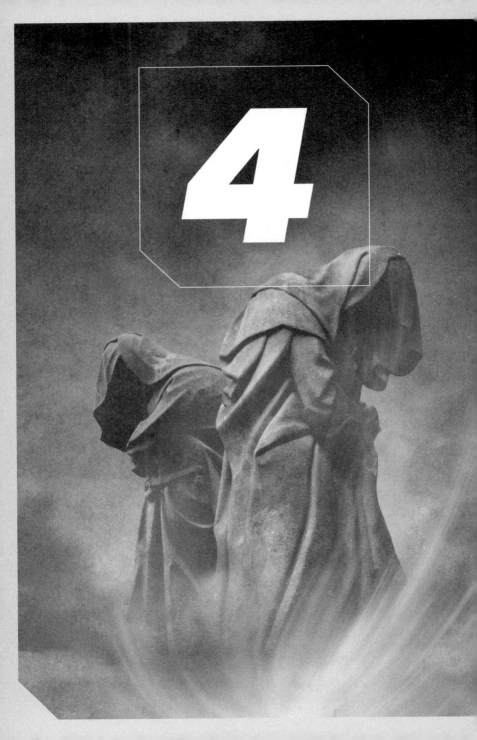

CHAPTER 4

Ghosts Throughout History

Pondering the Preponderance of Paranormal Activity

HERE WAS AT ATHENS A LARGE AND ROOMY VILLA, where in the dead of the night the rattling of chains was frequently heard. One night, a specter appeared to the homeowner. The apparition was extremely emaciated, with a long, matted beard and disheveled hair, and iron chains shackled to its hands and feet.

The terrified homeowner put the villa up for sale the very next day. It just so happened that the philosopher Athenodorus was in the market for a second home. The extraordinarily low listing price raised his suspicion. When he heard it was because the owner thought it was haunted, however, he laughed it off. Athenodorus was a learned man. He did not believe in ghosts and goblins.

His first week in the home passed without any disturbances. Then, late one night while philosophizing, he heard the telltale sound of iron dragging on the floor. It was distant at first, but approached nearer and nearer, slowly but surely.

Suddenly, a specter burst through his locked door!

Athenodorus glanced up at the hideous phantasm. It stood before him beckoning with a finger, like a person who calls another. Athenodorus in reply made a sign with his hand that it should wait for him to finish, and returned to his philosophical work.

~~~~

So begins one of the first ghost stories ever recorded, by Roman magistrate Pliny the Younger in a letter written nearly two thousand years ago. Despite Athenodorus's request that the ghost leave him alone, it rattled its chains morosely until the philosopher agreed to follow it into the backyard. The ghost pointed out a spot on the grass and let out a guttural moan. Athenodorus dug up the area, hoping to find some buried treasure. Instead, he found a rotting corpse. Athenodorus reluctantly paid to have the body given a proper burial at a graveyard, and the ghost never bothered him again.

At first glance, there's no reason to believe the story. For one thing, Pliny was relating a story passed down through the years, and you know how twisted a story gets just from one person to another in a game of telephone. Plus, how can a philosopher afford a second home? Erin took a philosophy class her junior year, taught by an assistant professor named Greg. He lived with three roommates. She might have gone on a couple of dates with him after the semester was over. Abby might have told Erin not to date one of her professors, especially one who was using his philosophy powers to manipulate her into thinking he was hot. BE WARNED: PHILOSOPHERS ARE MIND WIZARDS. They don't wear pointy hats or swing wands around, but they can trick you into picking up the tab for dinner at Weber's—and tickets for *The Net*, and a six-pack of Zima that neither of you touched—with nothing more than words.

So there are several reasons to be skeptical of Pliny's ghost story. Science demands evidence, not anecdotes. It is often said that the plural of "anecdote" is not "data." Every scientist worth her sodium chloride knows that.

However, is it not just as foolish to dismiss Pliny's tale—as well as the long historical record of ghost sightings—with one well-practiced Queen Elizabeth–like wave of the hand? Do we not then become Athenodorus, with our heads so buried in our work that we ignore the spectral visitors before our very eyes? As psychologist and metaphysical examiner William James pointed out, the sheer number of reports of paranormal phenomena throughout human history outweighs the anecdotal nature of the data. The prevalence of ghost stories across all cultures and time periods warrants serious consideration.

A GHOST BY ANY OTHER NAME

Ghosts are known by many names around the world:

- Apparition
- Appearance
- Bogey
- Essence
- Gidim

- Nightshade
- Phantasm
- Phantasma
- Phantom
- Phenomenon

- Presence
- Shade
- Shadow
- Sight
- Specter

- Spirit
- Spook
- Spud
- Vision
- Wraith

Source: Maureen Kemp. *Kemp's Spectral Field Guide*. New York: Doubleday, 1984.

Ancient History

Belief in ghosts predates the story of Athenodorus and his bothersome, incorporeal housemate by thousands of years. Prior to recorded history, stories of ghosts were passed by word of mouth—or, as historians call it, "the oral tradition." (STOP GIGGLING, ABBY.)

As a result, historical records from Mesopotamian cultures are kind of spotty. We don't know much about the political systems of Sumer, but we do know that women used oxen bladders for Spanx! Thankfully, we know just enough about ancient beliefs regarding ghosts to string a couple of sentences together.

As with most primitive cultures, superstitious beliefs were widespread. Sumerians, for instance, believed that when a person died, their soul descended into the netherworld to spend eternity as a "gidim." It didn't matter if you lived your life virtuously or not—everyone would eventually end up in an underground prison camp, toiling away with little to eat or drink. If surviving relatives didn't leave enough offerings on the grave of the deceased to ease their suffering, the gidim would return to torment the living. (Likely the origin of the modern-day tradition of "pouring one out for your homies.") However, despite the Sumerians' beliefs, actual ghost sightings were thought to be relatively rare.

Other Mesopotamian cultures, such as the Babylonians and ancient Egyptians, shared beliefs about the afterlife and ghosts similar to those of the Sumerians. Again, sightings were rare. Even after records started being written down, few ghost sightings were recorded in the kind of detail that would make them remotely useful to modern-day paranormal scholars such as ourselves. Or, if they do exist, we couldn't find them in Michigan's library.

The closest we have to a blow-by-blow account of a spirit manifestation from the pre-Greco-Roman era comes to us from the Old Testament. The story of the Witch of Endor takes place around 1,000 BC while Israel was at war with the Philistines. If Erin remembers it correctly from Sunday school, Israel's King Saul ordered a witch to conjure up the dead prophet Samuel, to see if Samuel could get God to confirm He had Israel's back in the war. (It's a rather roundabout plan.) The witch did a little hocus-pocus and BOOM! An old man wearing a robe emerged from the ground.

No, not Hugh Hefner—it was Samuel.

"Why have you disturbed me by bringing me up?" Samuel asked.

King Saul explained himself. The ghost listened rather impatiently, and then told the king that God was no longer backing King Saul and his army. "The Lord will deliver both Israel and you into the hands of the Philistines, and tomorrow you and your sons will be with me," the apparition said. Ouch.

As you would expect, there's plenty of theological debate surrounding this story. Was Samuel really a ghost, or just a trick of the devil? Scholars have long struggled to explain ghosts within the context of religion. As we'll see later, explaining them within the context of science has also been a struggle.

Classical Antiquity

The Greeks liberally ~~plagiarized~~ borrowed their beliefs about the afterlife from Mesopotamian culture. They also added several new twists. Depending upon their position in life and whether they pleased or angered the Greek gods, the dead could end up in Elysium (thumbs up!), the Fields of Punishment (thumbs down), or one of several other realms (thumbs to the side?). The Greeks still believed that ghosts—or "shades"—could return to the land of the living. For the first time, however, some heavy thinkers began questioning just how this whole paranormal business worked.

People who asked too many questions were called "philosophers." One such mind wizard stood tall above all others—and not just because he was six-and-a-half feet tall (but kind of for that reason too). In *Phaedo*, Plato argued that souls are neither created nor destroyed; they have always existed. We just can't see them. It's only after they've inhabited a body that they become "contaminated," thus rendering them visible to the naked eye when the body expires. That's how a shade becomes a shade. At least that's how Erin understands it, from her philosophy class with Greg. She doesn't want to call him to verify because we kind of need to finish this book by the end of the summer, and there's no guarantee Greg would shut up by then.

The Middle Ages and the Early Modern Period

Let's skip ahead a couple of hundred years, right past the Roman Pliny the Younger and into the Middle Ages. (You're not missing anything—the Romans were basically the same as the Greeks anyway, except they spoke Latin, had bowl cuts, and threw way better orgies.) We're also going to focus on Western cultures from here on out, because our foreign language skills are worse than our artistic ones.

Throughout the Middle Ages, people were dying left and right in Europe—from wars, from famine, from the Black Death, from . . . well, lots of things. Predictably, reports of paranormal phenomena rose steadily over the course of the Middle Ages as the death toll rose. "It seems that the spiritual world is moving closer to us, manifesting itself through visions and revelations," Gregory the Great wrote. (That's a totally different Greg than the one Erin went out with.)

Although previous cultures had mostly identified ghosts as the spirits of the deceased, some Europeans rejected this notion during the Middle Ages. Christian theologians, such as Saint Augustine, believed that ghostly apparitions weren't spirits of the dead. Instead, they suggested that parapercipients were experiencing visions caused by demons or angels. Recognize a ghost as a loved one? Mere trickery!

Following the Reformation, belief in ghosts split along party lines as Catholic theologians began floating the idea that spirits might be able to return to Earth after all. Protestants, meanwhile, remained steadfast that ghosts had nothing to do with the dead. Regardless, no one disputed that there was *something* out there going bump in the night, whether it be ghosts, demons, angels, or the occasional leprechaun.

Except for Louis Lavatar.

In *Of ghostes and spirites walking by nyght, and of strange noyses, crackes, and sundry forewarnynges*—the title goes on for another six lines, but you get the idea—the Protestant reformer cast doubt on eyewitness reports of all things paranormal, at least when it came to a certain gender. "Women, which for the most part are naturally given to fear more than men [. . .] do more often suppose they see or hear this or that thing, than men do," he wrote.

Perhaps Lavatar redeemed himself later in his book for all we know—we stopped reading his little manifesto (man-ifesto?). We do know one thing for sure: He might have been a long-winded sexist pig in serious need of spell-check, but Lavatar's words would prove eerily prophetic when the era of spiritualism rolled around.

MORE THAN JUST SPIRITS OF THE DEAD

The term "ghost" has traditionally referred to spirits of the deceased—mostly people, and occasionally animals. However, as you'll read in later chapters, this definition has been expanded over the years to include multiple classes of paranormal entities, including powerful interdimensional manifestations thought to be similar to the meddlesome demons and angels popular with Protestants in the Middle Ages.

The Spiritualist Era

Interest in the paranormal reached an all-time high in the nineteenth century with the advent of spiritualism. Unencumbered by established religious beliefs, self-styled "spiritualists" not only believed in ghosts, but they believed that communication with them was mainly the provenance of "mediums"—specially attuned individuals (usually women) who were emotionally and spiritually receptive to otherworldly dispatches, and could, on occasion, lure spirits from the other side. At its height, spiritualism had over eight million diehard adherents. Never before or since have ghosts been so popular in Western culture . . . and it all began with two young women.

Fifteen-year-old Margaret Fox and her sister, twelve-year-old Kate Fox (Figure 4.1), kicked off the spiritualist era when they opened a dialogue with a spirit haunting their cottage in 1848. The ghost, nicknamed "Mr. Splitfoot," never fully materialized in our world. Instead, he communicated with the girls through a novel method: When the girls asked him questions aloud, their friendly neighborhood ghost would "rap" his responses. Nobody could tell exactly where the noises came from, but the rapping was said to sound like someone was knocking on wood (though it may have very well been a primitive form of beatboxing, for all we know).

The Fox sisters started with simple yes or no questions. Rap once for "yes," twice for "no." They soon moved on to a Morse code–like system that allowed Mr. Splitfoot to spell out words. Curiously, the ghost—said to be the spirit of a vagabond buried deep in the Fox family's basement—would only

FIGURE 4.1.
The Fox sisters

communicate when the Fox sisters were around. The spirit told them that there were more spirits like him on the other side. Soon, they would make themselves known to other mediums around the world.

The young women took their show on the road. Mr. Splitfoot kindly followed them from city to city. The girls were lucky—not many ghosts would be quite so accommodating as to be treated like a sideshow act!

At any other point in Western history, the Fox sisters would have been burned at the stake or hung for communing with the dead in so public a fashion. However, the world was undergoing rapid change due to the Enlightenment. The sisters' traveling act drew huge crowds of the curious. Seemingly confirming the spirit's prophecy, dozens of mediums sprang up around the country. Not only could these imitators communicate with spectral manifestations in our world, but many boasted of the ability to contact any spirit, including those that had not yet "crossed over" into the material universe.

Spiritualism spread across the U.S. and Europe in the latter half of the nineteenth century like news of a snow day through a dorm. Who wouldn't be tempted by the thought of speaking with deceased loved ones just as easily as picking up a telephone? Mediums conducted dramatically staged "séances" to speak with spirits. These sessions were held in the dark or near-dark, with a small number of guests sitting around a table holding hands.

Spirits communicated through mediums not just via disembodied rapping, but through more direct methods like para-transferral embodiment. While possessed, mediums would speak, sing, and dance as if they were the spirits themselves. Ghosts even materialized during séances on occasion, leaving behind traces of spectral residue known as ectoplasm.

While a great number of people believed the mediums' claims, many were skeptical. Critics of the movement eventually found the smoking gun they'd been searching for, the one that they hoped would bring the public to their senses: Margaret Fox confessed that neither she nor her sister had ever communicated with ghosts. The ghostly rapping noises had been made by cracking their big toes. Their big, nasty, toes.

As additional mediums admitted to fraud or were proven to be hucksters, the movement slowly diminished in popularity. Some defenders cautioned against dismissing the entire movement based on a few bad apples. "I shall not commit the fashionable stupidity of regarding everything I cannot explain as a fraud," Carl Jung said in an address to the Society for Psychical Research.

The Fox sisters eventually recanted their confession, but the damage had been done. Although it's difficult to believe *every* medium was crooked—a few stood up to intense scrutiny from paranormal investigators, as you'll see in the next chapter—who can blame both the public and the spiritualists for losing faith?

Medium Tricks of the Trade

Apport: A solid object materialized during a séance, allegedly teleported from a different location or created by a spirit. One of the most famous instances of an apport appearing occurred during a séance with Eusapia Palladino, who shocked and amazed those in attendance by producing "a melon from nowhere." "Deports," in turn, disappear from séance rooms. While apports and deports were once thought to be signs of paranormal activity, they are now seen as fraud. You didn't *really* think that melon came from "nowhere," did you?

Automatic writing: A form of para-transferral embodiment, wherein a spirit directs the hand (or hands) of the possessed to write or type a message. Automatic writing was a popular method of spirit communication during the late 1800s, as mediums frequently entertained sitters with missives from well-known public figures and long-dead authors. Faking automatic writing is ridiculously easy. Magician Harry Houdini once sat with Jean Conan Doyle, the wife of Arthur Conan Doyle and a famed medium in her own right. She proceeded to deliver a twenty-three-page message from Houdini's deceased mother. While convincing in some of its facts, he was unconvinced of its authenticity. "It was written in English," he said, "a language which my mother never learned!"

Control: A spectral entity that acts as a spirit guide to the other side. Some mediums claim to speak with controls, that in turn locate other spirits that have not crossed over yet. Sometimes the spirit guide relays messages back and forth; sometimes the spirit guide drags them into our world, kicking and screaming. Whether or not controls actually have this ability is very much in question—they could be paranormal pranksters, pretending to pass messages back and forth. They could also be wholesale inventions on the part of mediums.

Direct voice phenomena (DVP): While many spirits possess mediums and speak through them, some ghosts speak without the aid of human vocal cords. Their voices seem to come from nowhere. During séances, mediums sometimes provide spirits with trumpets or horns to amplify their vocalizations, though this seems unnecessary (unless you're communicating with the ghost of Louis Armstrong).

Direct writing: Similar to automatic writing, although it appears without the use of the medium's hand. There are a few cases where direct writing has even appeared in the complete absence of a writing instrument!

Ectoplasm: An ethereal substance used by spirits to take physical shape during séances. Ectoplasm may also be responsible for phenomena such as DVP and direct writing, essentially allowing spirits to interact physically with this world. Ectoplasm will be discussed further in Chapter 6.

Xenoglossy: The act of writing or speaking in a language unknown to the practitioner; in paranormal circles, occurs when parapercipients are possessed by spirits.

Present Day

Few mediums exist today. Those who do are looked upon with suspicion. The same could also be said for anyone who has a paranormal experience these days, as Erin can attest to. Even though a majority of Americans believe in ghosts, good luck trying to get any of them to admit that in front of their coworkers or neighbors. Talking to an anonymous pollster is one thing; talking about ghosts in "polite society" is another. How ironic that the prudish Victorians were much more open to the paranormal!

Ghosts haven't gone anywhere. According to the latest Gallup survey, one in five people claims to have had a paranormal experience. Of course, the majority of "ghost sightings" are anything but. We readily acknowledge that. Even after adjusting the numbers to weed out alternative explanations for phenomena, however, the ratio of alleged paranormal incidents in society still shows a slight uptick from the spiritualist era (Figure 4.2).

The statistics don't lie: We are living in the most haunted period in recorded world history (due to factors we will explore in full in Chapter 12).

Parapercipient reports, filtered to remove probable naturalistic phenomena

Source: Hollis Queens, *Parapsychology; or, The Science of Psychical Phenomena* (New York: Harper and Row, 1989).

FIGURE 4.2.
Rising Worldwide Incidence of Paranormal Phenomena

Despite the ridicule that comes along with being associated with the para-normal, it would seem there's no other better time to be a metaphysical ex-aminer. Sadly, as we've discovered firsthand, few parapercipients are willing to open their doors to investigators. Much of the paranormal activity taking place remains unexamined.

Not that that's anything new. Every generation of ghost hunters has faced resistance. From skittish parapercipients to academic snobbery, the life of a metaphysical examiner has never been an easy one. In the next chapter, you'll meet the brave souls who paved the way for our present un-derstanding of the spirit world. But first, we need to visit the ladies' room. Let's fill and then empty the chamber pots and meet back here in five.

CHAPTER 5

Paranormal Investigators
A Look Back

S YOU PREPARE TO WORK IN ANY SCIENTIFIC field, it is important to know the names of those who came before you—something Professor Alderman drilled into us day in and day out. In this chapter, we'll introduce you to the fearless men and women who have dedicated their lives to further our collective understanding of the paranormal. These are the supernatural scientists who preceded us—the spectral warriors who marched through the darkness, flashlights and notebooks in hand, to investigate the unknown.

The Ghost Club

Although ghosts have been with us for thousands of years, it wasn't until the Enlightenment that scientifically minded intellectuals turned their attention to spirits of the dead. Paranormal investigation as we know it began in 1862 with London's Ghost Club. The Ghost Club's revolving roster was a virtual parapsychology Who's Who. Early members included Arthur Conan Doyle, computer pioneer Charles Babbage, and poet W. B. Yeats.

Although they professed to be paranormal investigators, the men in the Ghost Club actually investigated very few paranormal claims. Even during the spiritualist era, nobody wanted to open their doors to a bunch of spook hunters!

The early days of the Ghost Club more closely resembled a book club, with men just sitting around smoking cigars and drinking hot toddies. (That's what goes on at an all-male book club, right?) For whatever reason, the fine fellows in the Ghost Club didn't think women were equipped to handle the arduous task of discussing the paranormal. Full-torso apparitions didn't scare them. But cooties? Board up the windows!

Women were excluded from many such opportunities back in the 1800s, and had to make do with clubs such as the Ladies' Dining Society at the University of Cambridge. Would we rather sit around discussing ghosts, or go out to eat? Why not both? We don't have access to the Xerox right now,

FIGURE 5.1.
Offensive, right?

so Abby has drawn the original Ghost Club logo here (Figure 5.1).

Other ghost-hunting organizations soon popped up in England, including the London Dialectical Society and the Phasmatological Society. The most scientifically minded of the groups to form in this era was the Society for Psychical Research (SPR), cofounded by noted British intellectual Henry Sidgwick (Figure 5.2).

Henry Sidgwick (1838–1900) and Eleanor Sidgwick (1845–1936)

FIGURE 5.2.
Henry Sidgwick

Henry was headmaster at Newnham, a women's college at Cambridge, when he met Eleanor Balfour at a séance. Born to a wealthy British family, Eleanor had received a formal education at home which rivaled that of any public or private institution of the day. She had an analytical mind and was particularly fond of mathematics. The couple married in 1876, and Henry brought Mrs. Sidgwick (Figure 5.3) aboard at Newnham as vice principal.

FIGURE 5.3.
Eleanor Sidgwick

Their shared interest in the paranormal led to their involvement with the Society for Psychical Research. Henry became the group's first president. Eleanor, who would garner a reputation for being the more skeptical of the two, assisted with the publication of the SPR's official journal, *Phantasms of the Living.*

Together, the Sidgwicks approached the paranormal with a scientific view. This disappointed the spiritualists, who were, in Eleanor's words, "theological, not scientific." Eleanor sifted through thousands of ghost stories and paranormal experiences for her work with the SPR. She ultimately decided that most were complete bunk. She took no thrill in "pouring cold water over nine-tenths of our ghost stories," as she put it in the biography of her husband some years later.

Their fieldwork took them around the globe but yielded little in the way of empirical evidence. Still, the couple soldiered on. "I'm going to a haunted house," Henry once unenthusiastically wrote to a friend, "where I shall see no ghosts."

After Henry's premature death from cancer, Eleanor was elected president of the SPR. Henry's bearded ghost is said to haunt the halls of Newnham to this day. Eleanor, who passed away thirty-six years later, is presumably resting in peace.

William James (1842–1910)

With ghost-hunting clubs flourishing in England, Americans were keen to get in on the game as well. One of the earliest American paranormal investigators was the father of American psychology himself, William James (Figure 5.4). Similar to the Sidgwicks, James was a lifelong academic with a penchant for the paranormal. His accolades were impeccable: He was a professor of psychology at Harvard, as well as the author of the fledgling field's primary text, *The Principles of Psychology*.

FIGURE 5.4.
William James

While James considered himself a skeptic, he was open-minded about exploring the unknown. In 1884, he cofounded the American Society for Psychical Research. He envisioned the ASPR taking a middle road between "sentimentalism on the one side and dogmatizing ignorance on the other."

It would only take one airtight case to prove the existence of the paranormal, James reasoned. "If you wish to upset the law that all crows are black, you mustn't seek to show that no crows are; it is enough if you prove one single crow to be white," he said in a speech later transcribed in *Proceedings of the Society for Psychical Research*. "My own white crow is Ms. Piper."

"Ms. Piper" was one Leonora Piper (real name: Leonora Evelina Simonds), a famous American medium. Unlike others in her field, Piper was utterly without pretense. She didn't mess around with theatricality during her séances; she didn't even charge a fee for sitters (at least not early on in her career). In fact, she seemed quite astonished by her own abilities, which included contact with spirit guides that assumed control over her body. While James was skeptical of her at first, he came to believe that Piper's ability to communicate with ghosts (including the spirit of Abraham Lincoln) was genuine.

Despite his professed belief in Piper, neither James nor any of his colleagues could prove beyond a shadow of a doubt that she was the white crow. Without ectoplasm or other physical evidence of para-transferral embodiment, there could be no real proof the medium was being possessed by paranormal entities. Before James's death, he penned an essay for *The American Magazine* detailing his experiences as a paranormal investigator. "For twenty-five years I have . . . spent a good many hours (though far fewer than I ought to have spent) in witnessing (or trying to witness) phenomena," he wrote. "Yet I am theoretically no 'further' than I was at the beginning."

Twenty-five years of organized, scientifically backed investigations weren't long enough, he argued. What he needed—what the world needed—was more time. "We must expect to mark progress not by quarter-centuries but by half-centuries or whole centuries," James said.

Duncan MacDougall (1866–1920)

Toward the end of the first quarter-century of coordinated paranormal investigation, Dr. Duncan MacDougall conducted one of the most ostentatious experiments in scientific history.

In 1901, he placed six terminal tuberculosis patients onto an industrial scale and waited for them to die, clipboard in hand. As each patient expired, MacDougall recorded their weight. When the sixth and final patient passed away, a broad smile stretched across the doctor's face.

How could he not be excited? His hypothesis had been that if the human soul did, in fact, exist, then the loss of its mass should be observant upon the moment of death. According to his observations, four of his six patients exhibited a drop in weight at the exact moment of death. Dr. MacDougall calculated that the soul weighed approximately twenty-one grams (less than one-twentieth of a pound).

The *New York Times* broke the story in an exclusive. SOUL HAS WEIGHT, PHYSICIAN THINKS, the headline belted. No matter what you called the dissipating energy—soul or spirit—the doctor's experiment was a potentially huge step in our understanding of the metaphysical world. Up until MacDougall's controlled experiment, no one had proven the existence of spirit energy. His findings were hailed as the empirical evidence that paranormal investigators had been searching for.

Unfortunately, subsequent researchers called MacDougall's methods into question. They suggested the weight loss could have been from moisture loss through either pores or the final exhalation of breath. Disappointingly, his results were never repeated. It's probably for the best, too: There are much less drastic ways to drop one-twentieth of a pound.

Marie Curie (1867-1934) and Pierre Curie (1859-1906)

Besides James and MacDougall, a few other brave scientists decided to risk their academic careers tangling with the paranormal. Sir J. J. Thomson, discoverer of the electron, joined the Society for Psychical Research. If electrons were floating around in the air all around us, he reasoned, what else was out there beyond the reach of current scientific technology? Chemist William Crookes gave paranormal investigation a spin, although his skeptically minded colleagues attributed his interest in ghosts to mental illness brought on by repeated exposure to the chemical element he discovered, thallium. And Nobel Prize–winning French physiologist Charles Richet wasn't just an SPR member—he served as president. Even Marie and Pierre Curie (Figure 5.5) stepped their toes into the world of paranormal investigation.

Hot on the heels of their shared win of the Nobel Prize in Physics, the husband-and-wife researchers participated in a series of séances put on by the SPR, featuring noted medium Eusapia Palladino in Paris in 1905. "It was very interesting, and really the phenomena that we saw appeared inexplicable as trickery—tables raised from all four legs, movement of objects from a distance, hands that pinch or caress you, luminous apparitions," Pierre wrote.

While Pierre went on to state that such tricks could be performed by magicians, the Curies also saw enough during their sessions to convince them that further investigation was needed. They hoped to link the

FIGURE 5.5.
Pierre (left) and Marie Curie (right)

worlds of the physical and the psychical, perhaps explaining the paranormal through radioactivity—or vice versa. "There is here, in my opinion, a whole domain of entirely new facts and physical states in space of which we have no conception," Pierre wrote to his friend, Louis Georges Gouy, in the spring of 1906. "These phenomena really exist and it is no longer possible for me to doubt it."

Tragically, Pierre was killed in a street accident less than a week after

FIGURE 5.6.
Arthur Conan Doyle (left) and Harry Houdini (right)

posting the letter. "I lost my beloved Pierre, and with him all hope and all support for the rest of my life," Marie later recalled. They were more than husband and wife; they were partners in the lab. Without him, she was lost. She picked herself up, however, taking over Pierre's chair at the University of Paris to become the first female professor at the university. In 1911, she was awarded a second Nobel Prize, this time for her discovery of the elements radium and polonium.

Marie Curie never followed up on her late husband's grandiose plans to methodically investigate the paranormal. Given the many ways mediums of the day were capable of tricking sitters, it was a wise decision. To catch a trickster, you had to be one yourself.

Enter the Great Houdini.

Harry Houdini (1874-1926)

Besides being one of the twentieth century's greatest illusionists, Houdini was also an avid metaphysical examiner who publicly investigated paranormal claims. Although he started out with an open mind about the paranormal, the number of fraudulent mediums he encountered led him to sour on the idea of ghosts being real.

Many of the mediums he investigated were using the same sorts of tricks magicians used to entertain audiences. Houdini took this as a personal insult. Magicians entertained, rather than deceived, their audiences. Toward the end of his life, Houdini embarked on a nationwide crusade to bust fake mediums. "Tell the people that all I am trying to do is to save them from being tricked in their grief and sorrows," he wrote in *The Christian Register.*

Houdini's on-again, off-again friend Arthur Conan Doyle (Figure 5.6) doubted the magician had any genuine interest in proving the existence of the paranormal, outside of the publicity his debunking work brought him. "His theoretical knowledge of the subject was limited," Doyle wrote after Houdini passed away. "For though he possessed an excellent library, it was, when I inspected it, neither catalogued nor arranged." Sick burn, Doyle.

Just because Houdini was dead didn't mean he couldn't hear the shot his old frenemy had fired. Though Houdini remained a skeptic to the end of his life, he had prepared for the possibility that he would return as a ghost. He left a secret code with his wife—that way, she would know if she was being deceived by a medium claiming to speak on his behalf.

For ten straight years following his death, Bess Houdini held an annual séance on Halloween, attempting to reach out to him. Her husband never answered her calls. When *Newsweek* asked why she finally gave up on his spirit, Bess replied, "Ten years is long enough to wait for any man."

Harry Price (1881-1948)
and Kathleen M. Goldney (1895-1992)

During the early part of the twentieth century, the public began to give up on the long wait for proof of the paranormal as well. Still, while interest in the paranormal was on the decline, investigators and researchers continued their work on both sides of the pond. Harry Price (Figure 5.7) joined the SPR in 1922 and quickly made a name for himself as a self-styled "ghost hunter."

In contrast to many of his peers at the SPR, Price had no higher-level educational background to draw upon—like Houdini, he was a gifted magician with a flair for the flamboyant. Unlike Houdini, he wasn't such a hardline skeptic. Or maybe he was. Price's views on the paranormal flip-flopped so often, it is impossible to say what he truly thought. "There is no scientific proof of survival," he admitted in his bestselling memoir, *Confessions of a Ghost-Hunter*, before going on to recount ghost story after ghost story. According to his critics, his theories were the worst kind of popular tripe, his methods were sloppy, and his conclusions highly questionable.

The public, of course, ate it all up.

While the previous generation of ghost hunters had been stigmatized by their chosen profession, Price became something more than a mere academic castoff: He became a celebrity. For a time, at least, his antics temporarily rekindled the public's flagging interest in spooks and specters.

Despite his lack of academic training, Price had a keenly scientific mind. He carried a notebook with him on investigations and stakeouts so that he could record his observations in real time, instead of relying on his memory. Price used battery-powered flashlights, which were invented around the turn of the century. He also used a thermograph to note changes in temperature. He even carried a portable camera with infrared film.

In 1925, Price founded the National Laboratory of Psychical Research, which later became the University of London Council for Psychical Investigation. He reformed the defunct Ghost Club and, for good measure, revolutionized it by letting women in for the first time in 1938. As reported by Rosemary Guiley in *The Encyclopedia of Ghosts and Spirits*, Price described his vision for the all-new Ghost Club as a "body of extremely skeptical men **and women** who get together every few weeks to hear the latest news of the psychic world and to discuss every facet of the paranormal" (emphasis ours).

FIGURE 5.7.
Harry Price

Price's assistant, Kathleen M. Goldney, became one of the Society for Psychical Research's top paranormal investigators and later vice president of the organization. Goldney is reputed to have had a well-tuned b.s. detector. "She possesses a steam-roller personality, capable of crushing any witness," said Nandor Fodor, author of *An Encyclopaedia of Psychic Science*.

In fact, it's possible she was a little too harsh on parapercipients. "An examinee would have to have a tremendous strength of mind to emerge from three or four hours of cross-examination by her without being brainwashed," Fodor wrote in the journal *Tomorrow*. "She is eminently capable of convincing almost any witness that he did not see what he saw."

Goldney, rumored to have been romantically involved with her mentor at one time, later coauthored a scathing indictment of his investigatory techniques for the SPR that left Price's reputation in tatters. You know what they say about a ghost hunter scorned.

J. B. Rhine (1895-1980) and Louisa Rhine (1890-1983)

A push to study the paranormal on college campuses happened in the early part of the present century, spearheaded in part by Price. One of the few successful attempts to establish a paranormal studies department occurred at Duke University, where Dr. J. B. Rhine founded the highly influential Parapsychology Laboratory in 1930. His wife, Dr. Louisa Rhine, later joined him at Duke.

Botanists by trade, the Rhines became obsessed with the paranormal after attending an Arthur Conan Doyle lecture on spirit communication. J.B. put his academic training to use studying the paranormal, although he never called it by that name. He positioned paranormal studies as an experimental branch of psychology. The term he coined—parapsychology—is still in use today, even though it's clear the paranormal has more in common with physics than psychology.

The bulk of the Rhines' work at the Parapsychology Laboratory focused not on ghosts, but on forms of extrasensory perception such as clairvoyance and telekinesis. By proving such phenomena under controlled conditions in a lab, J.B. believed he could pave the way toward research of spirits. After all, if the human mind could be shown to have dominion outside the known bounds of space and time, then it opened the door for the cognizant human spirit to transcend the physical universe—and with it, death.

The lab's most famous trials seemed to confirm its director's suspicions that mind reading and other psychical phenomena were real. In several published studies, the Rhines and their colleagues demonstrated that certain highly attuned individuals could guess what was on hidden cards in higher percentages than mere chance could explain.

There was a brief moment in time when it looked like the Rhines' work was paying off in terms of mainstream acceptance. The American Association for the Advancement of Science recognized parapsychology as an official branch of psychology in 1969. In 1973, *Psychology Today* suggested that parapsychology was "an idea whose time has come." *U.S. News & World*

Report echoed the call, stating, "Slowly but steadily, parapsychology is edging toward scientific respectability after years of lurking on the fringes."

Unfortunately, just as it looked like things were on the upswing, a backlash occurred within the scientific establishment. Parapsychology fell victim to its own success. The famous Duke University trials came under intense scrutiny. While outright fraud was not found, lapses in methodology and missing records of vital data all but consigned the lab to the scrap heap of history, at least according to critics. Nobody outside of the Parapsychology Laboratory has ever been able to replicate any of the most extraordinary trial results.

The Ongoing Quest

While many historical ghost-hunting organizations are still around, most paranormal investigators work on their own or within smaller, regional groups, far outside of academia. Those within the scientific community who do come out as believers are branded as "sheep" by colleagues. "My colleagues make sheep noises at me in the halls," University of Northeastern California professor of biology Jason Haley said of his own experience. "Bah. Bah. Baaaaaaaaaaaaaaah."

However, there is hope. Many advances in scientific fields have come out of left field. Did Einstein announce his general theory of relativity in some boring scientific journal? Okay, he did, but that's beside the point. What we're trying to say is that the paranormal will continue to be relegated to second-class status in the scientific community for the foreseeable future. You think that's going to stop us from publishing our work?

If you're reading these words, the answer should be obvious. (If it's not, we're a little worried about you.)

Let us say finally that we're eternally grateful for those trailblazers who have come before us, even though William James's white crow remains at large. That's to be expected. "When we explore uncharted territory to the limits of knowledge, we have little guidance; so we are forced to explore in many directions," Victor J. Stenger writes in *Physics and Psychics*. "Most turn out to be blind alleys. Failure is more common than success."

Although it's true that no ghost hunter has ever "caught" a ghost, their blind alleys and failures have contributed greatly to our current understanding of the nature of spectral entities, which we will discuss in the next chapter.

CHAPTER 6

A Scientific Exploration
Introducing Spectral Field Theory

THE TRADITIONAL VIEW OF THE PARANORMAL IS ROOTED in the belief that there are phenomena beyond our senses, phenomena that the laws of nature cannot account for. According to this view, there are two separate worlds: the physical world, which consists of perceptible matter, and the metaphysical world, which consists of paranormal phenomena that break natural laws.

Take ghosts, for instance. They are said to appear out of thin air, apparently violating the Law of Conservation of Mass. They are known to possess both tangible and intangible properties, at times physically interacting with our world and at other times passing through walls. Since scientists can't account for the behavior of such entities using natural laws, they've all but dismissed the paranormal as a physical impossibility.

You know what else breaks the laws of the natural world? Quantum mechanics. Many of the laws governing the smallest particles run contrary to the laws governing the macroworld. Scientists have even gone so far as to label the behavior of particles "spooky." Yet quantum theory is accepted as mainstream physics, while the similarly spooky world of natural law–breaking paranormal phenomena is laughed off as a joke by conventionalists.

The time has come to upend the existing paradigm. We believe the metaphysical can finally be explained—using (you guessed it) quantum mechanics. If we were associate professors at some stuffy university, we'd probably be fired for what we're about to suggest. Luckily for you, neither of us has a job in academia currently! Or any job. Or much of a life beyond our passion for proving the paranormal.

Spectral Field Theory

The paranormal investigators we introduced you to in the previous chapter spent a lot of time in the field, searching for ghosts. While physical evidence will one day confirm the existence of the paranormal, until then we must rely on the theoretical.

If you've never heard of Spectral Field Theory, don't worry—it's so new it's still got that new theory smell. It's our own theory. You're hearing about it here first because no journal has the ovaries to print it. *Nature* is the lone place that returned our query letter, and that was only because there was postage due.

Thanks to the physicists who constructed quantum field theory, we know the elementary particles at the root of the Standard Model of physics: quarks, leptons, gluons, photons, Z bosons, W bosons, and Higgs. However, the Standard Model, which governs the fundamental laws of nature, cannot account for the paranormal.

That's where Spectral Field Theory comes in. Our observations, when coupled with those of generations of paranormal researchers and theoretical physicists, leave us no choice but to postulate the existence of a new gauge field, hereafter known as the "spectral ether."

Localized excitation of this ether by unknown, interdimensional entities in the form of spectral particles results in a spectral foam (or "ectoplasm"). What is commonly referred to as a manifestation can be understood as physical phenomena in which significant coupling exists between spectral and Standard Model particles. Therefore, the—

Actually, strike that. It's a lot easier to explain if we just write out the equation.

SPECTRAL FIELD DYNAMICS, AS PREDICTED BY THE YATES-GILBERT EQUATION

The Yates-Gilbert Equation can be written in Lagrangian terms as:

$$\int_a \sin x \, dx = -\cos x \big|_a = \cos b - \cos a ; \, x \cos a$$

Running this through the Euler-Lagrange limiting equation, we get:

$$\int_a \sin x \, dx = -\cos x \big|_a = \cos b - \cos a ; \, x \cos a \int_1^2 x^2 \, dx = \frac{x^3}{5}\Big|_1^2 = \frac{2^3 - 1^3}{3} = 8 - 1 = 7; \, \frac{\ln 8}{\ln a}$$

Now, consider a space-time n-dimensional target manifold, with local coordinates as follows:

$$\int_a \sin x \, dx = -\cos x \big|_a = \cos b - \cos a ; \, x \cos a \int_1^2 x^2 \, dx = \frac{x^3}{5}\Big|_1^2 = \frac{2^3 - 1^3}{3} = 8 - 1 = 7; \, \frac{\ln 8}{\ln a}$$

$$x + 2\,Arth\,t = \ln\left(\frac{1+t}{1-t}\right)\frac{8}{a}\frac{(\sqrt{2}-\sqrt{3})^2 + 2\sqrt{6}}{(\sqrt{6}-1)(\sqrt{6}+1)} = \frac{1}{2}$$

This is the spectral gauge field, which can be expanded as:

$$\int_a \sin x \, dx = -\cos x \big|_a = \cos b - \cos a ; \, x \cos a \int_1^2 x^2 \, dx = \frac{x^3}{5}\Big|_1^2 = \frac{2^3 - 1^3}{3} = 8 - 1 = 7; \, \frac{\ln 8}{\ln a}$$

$$x + 2\,Arth\,t = \ln\left(\frac{1+t}{1-t}\right)\frac{8}{a}\frac{(\sqrt{2}-\sqrt{3})^2 + 2\sqrt{6}}{(\sqrt{6}-1)(\sqrt{6}+1)} = \frac{1}{2}\int\frac{e^x \, de^x}{\sqrt[4]{e^x+1}^9}\int f(x)\,dx = F(x)\big|^b$$

where f is a partial derivative of F, when PKE = PKE(x). The covariance of the Lagrangian can be modified by the coupling agent Y, where Y = any Standard Model particle. Ectoplasm is generated when the following variables are met:

As you can see, the math is pretty much self-explanatory. Now let's take a closer look at the components of Spectral Field Theory, beginning with psychokinetic energy.

Psychokinetic Energy

If the human spirit survives death, it is unlikely to be measurable as a drop in weight. (Sorry, Dr. MacDougall.) If the soul had any mass to it at all, we would surely have incontrovertible scientific proof of it by this point. Therefore, if some remnant of the human spirit exists following death, it must be composed of spectral particles without material substance. We have no idea how many different types of elementary spectral particles there are, or how they interact. While we're operating under the assumption of basic Lagrangian density here, there may be other subatomic dynamics at work. You understand what we're saying, though.

Spectral particles—which we collectively call "psychokinetic energy," or PKE for short—have no physical substance, at least not as we conceive of it in the three-dimensional natural world. Much like dark matter and dark energy, this spirit energy is currently undetectable using scientific equipment. It exists only in theory. With recent advances in hadron colliders, we may not be far off from detecting such particles, but we're not there yet.

Despite the spectral field dynamics predicted by the Yates-Gilbert Equation, we're still left with several questions. If we had the means to measure it—a PKE meter, if you will—would we detect PKE inside living bodies? If so, why doesn't it interact with Standard Model particles until it's left the body? Does it have something to do with the "contamination" Plato spoke about? And how can Tomorrow's Teriyaki legally sell "crabmeat rangoons" without even a trace of crab, imitation or otherwise? And just what the hell is "imitation crab," exactly? Don't tell us there are fish out there pretending to be crabs, just to confuse fishermen. Alas, such pressing questions must remain unanswered for now.

The Spectral Ether: Welcome to the Other Side

Very few people have clinically died and been revived. Those who have, however, frequently claim to have had near-death experiences (NDEs). After being resuscitated, near-death experients report having "left" their bodies. As evidence, some experients undergoing operations have described details of hospital rooms—including specialized tools and specific personnel they should have no knowledge of—in impressive detail. While NDEs vary wildly, most experients agree on one point: They remember floating down a dark tunnel toward a bright light. We posit that this light is a higher dimension.

Everyone is familiar with the first three dimensions—length, height, and depth. If you're not, then you might want to just, uh, look at the world around you? According to Einstein's special theory of relativity, which has prevailed over physics for nearly one hundred years, there's also a fourth dimension: time. Superstring theory posits at least six additional dimensions, all imperceptible to current scientific methods of measurement. Possibly ten. You might even go one better, all the way to eleven. In fact, theoretical physicists have used superstring theory to hypothesize an infinite number of universes and timelines—the "multiverse" theory. When we talk about spirits, however, we're only talking about one of these universes: the spectral ether.

This alternate dimension of mysterious spectral particles goes by many names: the other side, the spirit world, the afterlife, the unseen world, the netherworld, Elysium,

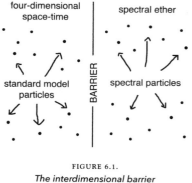

FIGURE 6.1.
The interdimensional barrier
Abby, created in MS Paint

the heavens. While some have claimed to have visited it, nobody really knows for certain what it holds. That's because it lies beyond our senses on the other side of an interdimensional barrier. This invisible thin wall is like a pane of glass that separates our world from the next (Figure 6.1).

The Durable but Not Impenetrable Barrier

Much like light is unable to escape the gravitational field of a black hole, spirits of the dead are unable to avoid being drawn through the barrier into the spectral ether. (We're talking about the dead now, not the near-dead.) For the majority of spirits, this journey is one-way. Once they've crossed over, that's it.

However, sometimes they come back.

The return trip isn't easy—it's damn near impossible. The true ghost sighting is rare for this very reason. But "near impossible" isn't the same as "impossible." No matter how durable the barrier between dimensions is, it is not impenetrable. Spirits of the deceased (as well as the occasional interdimensional entity) make the trip far more often than we'd like.

Think of the barrier as a diaphragm. As birth control, diaphragms are mostly effective. They block entry to the uterus, acting as barriers to conception. However, even when used properly, every year six out of a hundred women will get pregnant while using diaphragms—decent odds, if you're in the lucky 94 percent. But NOT COOL if you're one of the other gals. The pill is more reliable, when taken correctly—up to 99.9 percent effective.

Too bad there isn't a pill for our universe! We have to rely on the barrier betwixt worlds. The good news is that it's *more effective* than the birth control pill. Based on the number of ghost sightings out of the total number of deceased on this planet throughout history, we calculate the barrier is 99.99996 percent effective.

That's not bad—in fact, it's rather fantastic, from a statistical standpoint. Unfortunately, that equates to tens of thousands of "accidents" over the years.

Structural Fluctuations in the Barrier

The spectral ether can best be imagined as a prison. Suppose a suspect is arrested and convicted for murdering his wife and her lover. (Let's pretend he didn't do it.) The judge sentences him to life behind bars, at which point he is transported straight to the prison grounds. After nineteen long years, however, the prisoner manages to escape via a tunnel in his cell hidden behind a poster of Raquel Welch. Eventually, the prisoner is recaptured and returned to Shawshank State Prison. Unless we're talking about Andy Dufresne, in which case he's never caught because he's chilling on a beach in Mexico with MORGAN MF-ING FREEMAN, BABY!!!!!

Sorry. We just watched *Shawshank Redemption* last night.

Like the walls of Andy's cell, the barrier is weaker in some spots than in others. Paranormal experts have long floated the theory that ghosts do not appear at wholly random spots around the globe. If you look at maps of ghost sightings, they frequently match up with ancient sacred sites and

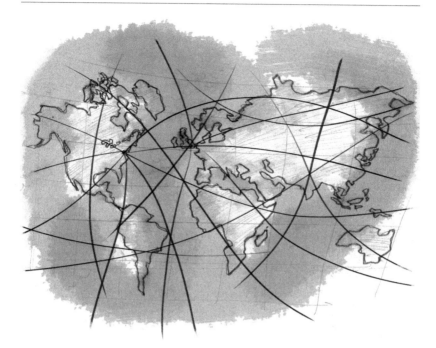

FIGURE 6.2.
Elis Ley Line Map

reported paranormal happenings from times past. These "paranormal hot spots" are thought to be weakened points between the dimensions. They can be connected around the globe using a loose network of straight lines called "ley lines." They are known by different names around the world, such as "spirit lines" (Peru) and "dragon lines" (China).

Using a comprehensive database of paranormal phenomena, Stanford physicist and professor Marcus Elis created a modern-day map of ley lines in the 1980s (Figure 6.2). According to Elis's calculations, cities such as New York and London have rich histories of the paranormal for a reason: multiple ley lines converge within their boundaries. This is known as the Elis Vortex Theory. Such ley-line vortices act as magnets for the paranormal.

Additionally, folklore holds that the barrier between life and death fluctuates in strength throughout the day. Ancient superstition states that when a cock crows at dawn, ghosts must return to the other side until nightfall. While more ghosts are reported during the evening, it's not clear this has anything to do with "cocks crowing." It could be that we are more perceptive when the sun is down, the TV is turned off, and we're in bed with a good book. People are certainly more sensitive to the paranormal at night—as the saying goes, "During the day, I don't believe in ghosts. At night, I'm a little more open-minded." (We're not sure who said that, exactly. Erin says it was Benjamin Franklin, but Abby swears it was Nicolas Cage.)

Ghosts are also said to be more active during certain times of the year—in particular, on Halloween, when the barrier is said to be at its weakest. While more parapercipients report experiencing phenomena on October 31 than on other days by a wide margin, it's likely because people are primed to expect the paranormal. Everybody believes in the paranormal on Halloween. It's just like people who don't normally drink getting falling-down drunk on New Year's Eve. It's amateur hour.

The Ectomaterialistic Nature of Ghosts

But, you ask, if spectral particles are truly invisible to our senses, how is it that thousands upon thousands of parapercipients have reported seeing and hearing ghosts over the years?

To which we pose another question (this time directed your way): Why has no one ever seen a ghost *leaving* a body? Surely, if ghosts were nothing more than disembodied human spirits, some doctor somewhere would have at least reported seeing a ghost exiting a newly deceased patient! This is one of the eternal mysteries surrounding the paranormal, and we are pleased to say WE KNOW THE ANSWER.

When a parapercipient sees a "ghost," they are actually seeing an ectoplasmic avatar animated by PKE. Ectoplasm is a spectral foam generated through interactions between PKE and Standard Model particles when spirits cross back through the barrier. According to the mathematical framework we've developed for Spectral Field Theory, negatively charged ectoplasm is in turn utilized by spirits to physically interact within the three-dimensional framework of our world. To the naked eye, such manifestations may appear either transparent or opaque, depending on their density.

Philosopher Emanuel Swedenborg is credited with the discovery of ectoplasm in 1744. When he was fifty-six, he began hearing the voices of spirits and angels. Since he was a respected Swedish intellectual—and a man—nobody dared call him "Ghost Guy." In his very first vision, he spoke of "a kind of vapour steaming from the pores of my body. It was a most visible watery vapour and fell downwards to the ground upon the carpet." The ionized eco-matter transmogrified into spectral rats, which scurried off in all directions.

Ectoplasm made a big splash (pun intended) during the latter half of the nineteenth century, when it began appearing at spiritualist séances as a mucus-like substance. Physical mediums were said to excrete the spectral foam not just from their pores, but from every orifice.

Including that one.

And that one.

Unfortunately, every sample of ectoplasm tested so far by paranormal investigators has been found to be some other substance, such as wet cheesecloth. One medium was even busted for using livestock entrails (YUCK). Although it gets a bad rap due to its association with fraudulent mediums, most paranormal experts, such as Maureen Kemp (whom you'll meet in the next chapter), are confident that ectoplasm exists. We're inclined to follow her lead. And not just because we wrote her a fan letter and she responded that she'd blurb our book.

Getting our hands on ectoplasm and testing it in a lab might be the only way we're going to make the breakthrough necessary for parapsychology to be taken seriously by the scientific establishment. It won't be easy, though—according to Spectral Field Theory, the rate of decay for low- to medium-density ionized eco-matter all but guarantees that ectoplasm dissipates in a matter of minutes. Higher density spectral manifestations, while rarer, should provide more substantive samples of ectoplasmic residue.

The Reasons Spirits of the Dead Return

Based upon the malevolent actions of specters reported in most ghost sightings, we aren't visited by many peaceful spirits. The calm spirits appear to all just be chilling out on the other side, while only the most desperate or angry make the trip back to our world.

Just as only the most determined sperm find their way past diaphragms, it appears a certain amount of grit and determination is required for spirits to find their way through the barrier. Even if spirits aren't motivated by hostile

Ghosts: Never Nude?

"Even if you are disposed to believe in spirits, how can you account for the clothes they wear when they appear before your startled vision?" early-twentieth-century feminist author Charlotte Perkins Gilman once asked. The question has dogged believers and nonbelievers alike since the beginning of time. Here are a few theories:

- **Ghosts are as modest as the living.** "Of course they are clothed," Arthur Conan Doyle once wrote, suggesting that ghosts would find it just as unpleasant as parapercipients would if they were to make appearances in their birthday suits.
- **Ghosts are "projections" formed in the parapercipient's mind.** We're not talking about hallucinations here, at least not as we understand them. According to this theory, all spectral entities exist as little more than balls of light. Our brains interpret them as humanoid apparitions. What to one person looks like their grandfather may appear to another as the Virgin Mary. A fascinating take, but the physics boggle the mind.
- **It's cold on the other side.** Alexandre Inman, writing in *It's Your Afterlife: A Handbook for Lost Souls*, says that the temperature registers in the negative double digits in the spirit world—almost as cold as Michigan in February. There is a long tradition in some parts of the world of friends and relatives leaving garments out on graves to clothe freezing spirits, although the gesture is seen as more symbolic than practical.
- **Ghosts appear exactly as they did at the time of their death.** Of the various theories, this one holds the least ions for us. Some spirits appear as they did earlier in life, and not at life's end. Besides, if this theory were true, wouldn't more ghosts appear in hospital gowns?

intentions, they're bound to pick up some interdimensional road rage along their arduous journey.

The reasons ghosts return are as varied as the forms they take on Earth. According to William Ambrose Collins, author of *The Great Book of Other Realms*, spirits make the journey

- To seek revenge, especially if they were murdered
- To request their remains be buried properly, so they can rest in peace
- To say good-bye, offer comfort, or give warning to a loved one
- To confess their sins . . . or to commit new ones

- To guard over hidden treasure or assist their heirs in finding it
- Just for the hell of it ("mischievous in life, mischievous in death")

As you can see, most reasons are related to unfinished business. Ghosts, just like Abby's ex-boyfriend Sam, seem to be obsessed with getting "closure." Whatever that is.

The vast majority of ghosts presumably get their closure and return to the spectral ether. We assume this because most ghost sightings resolve on their own, without any intervention on the part of ghost hunters, exorcists, or the like. Perhaps spirits return of their own volition, finding their way back the same way they came, through weakened spots in the barrier. It's also possible they are involuntarily drawn back by the same unseen forces that initially sucked them through to the other side.

When spirits exit our world, there's a remote chance they also leave some ectoplasm behind as residue. Until we find and test some of that ionized eco-matter in the lab, we're really just relying on educated guesses as to how all of this works. Theories can only take us so far.

Spectral Field Theory also doesn't tell us anything about the sentience, intelligence, or malevolence of paranormal entities, let alone the physical forms that manifestations may take. For that, we will need to consult the spectral anthropologists in the next chapter.

7

Unnatural Anthropology
The Evolution of
Supernatural Taxonomy

N THE PAST COUPLE OF CHAPTERS, WE'VE INTRODUCED YOU to spirits, spooks, and specters—all different names for the entities we call "ghosts." However, not all ghosts are created equal. Some ghosts appear as dim balls of light; others as entirely opaque humanoids. Mistaking a Class II repeater for a floating free-roaming vapor is like calling iceberg lettuce "kale." They're both green, leafy vegetables, but one goes on a burger and the other goes in the compost.

The kale, not the free-roaming vapor. Don't ever toss a Class II in the compost.

Classifying the biological world is difficult enough. To continue with our hamburger-topping theme, consider tomatoes for a moment. Are they vegetables or fruit? How would you like to be the scientist who had to make that call?!! At least there's enough physical evidence for the existence of tomatoes. When you're dealing with the paranormal, direct observation is maddeningly elusive. Evidence is woefully lacking. There are very few dependable photographic accounts to rely on, let alone any sort of fossil record.

That's where the supernatural anthropologists in this chapter come in. Instead of chasing ghosts, they have spent their time examining ghost stories recorded by cultural historians and cataloging the reports filed by paranormal investigators in order to do the unthinkable: make order out of chaos.

Archibald Dutton's *Systema Unnaturae*

Among the earliest attempts to classify the paranormal was one made by prize-winning British equestrian Archibald Dutton (Figure 7.1). Born in 1742 in Haslingden, the child prodigy went to the New College at Hackney to study medicine at the age of thirteen. He graduated in two years and immediately went to work as a physician in London.

They say practice makes perfect, but Dutton was, in fact, a terrible doctor. He accidentally killed more patients than he accidentally saved. Which makes total sense, AS HE WAS ONLY FIFTEEN. After six painful months, he retired from the medical profession and became a man of letters (that's what writers were called back then—even women, if they were allowed to write).

In 1787, Dutton published *Systema Unnaturae*, the first major scientific assessment of paranormal phenomena. Although Dutton's medical schooling had done little to prepare him for such a study, he had plenty of experience with spirits of the dead based on the unintentional body count he'd amassed during his time as a working physician.

In between tales of his dead patients coming back to haunt him, Dutton included a selection of ghost stories plagiarized from earlier (now lost) works of the paranormal. (He also, bizarrely,

FIGURE 7.1.
Archibald Dutton

penned an entire chapter on the history of the horse as a means of transportation, which not even his biographers have been able to get through.) None of that matters, thankfully. What does matter is the classification system found in the appendix of his book.

Dutton sorted spirits into seven different categories: *bogeys, fantomas,* *wheaties**, *vapours, spectres, poltergeists,* and *daemons.* Unfortunately, he did not adequately explain his methodology within the text. Are the ghosts arranged by size and shape, or by some other as-yet-undiscovered logic known only to Dutton?

SYSTEMA UNNATURAE

I. BOGEYS

II. FANTOMAS

III. WHEATIES

IV. VAPOURS

V. SPECTRES

VI. POLTERGEISTS

VII. DAEMONS

Source: Archibald Dutton. Systema Unnaturae. London: J. W. Bouton, 1787.

Despite the obfuscation (which may very well have been intentional, given Dutton's lack of scholarly acumen), no one dared challenge his taxonomy of spirits for the next hundred and fifty years. This was primarily due to how Dutton met his end: at the sharp end of an axe. His crime: running afoul of the Blasphemy Act of 1697. The system of spirits outlined in *Systema Unnaturae* appeared to conflict with the Church of England's teachings—we say "appeared to," because no one, not even King George III, could make sense of Dutton's work. Especially that chapter on horses.

Though the Act of Parliament banning blasphemy was rarely enforced, Dutton's refusal to renounce his views (or even clarify them) earned him a date with the executioner. The aristocracy, intending to make an example of him, had him publicly beheaded—the first execution of its kind in decades. Dutton's head rolled off the chopping block and into the Haslingden town square, where children kicked it around the cobblestone streets, leading some to wryly credit Archibald Dutton with the invention of soccer.

Vernon Heiss's Occult Manifestation Index

By the 1920s, Western governments had cooled off somewhat on the whole "executing people for blasphemy" concept. After investigators unmasked most famous mediums of the day as frauds, the public's appetite for the paranormal waned during the latter part of the Roaring Twenties. Besides, people just wanted to drink and have a good time, not dwell on the dearly

---

* *In the eighteenth century, wheaties were partial-torso apparitions that haunted fields. There's no connection to the breakfast cereal Wheaties . . . THAT WE KNOW OF. (Cue ominous music.)*

departed. While most of his colleagues were busy drinking bootleg
liquor in speakeasies, Vernon Heiss
(Figure 7.2) was hunkered down
in his Upper West Side apartment
with a typewriter, pounding out
a 1,007-page guide to spooks and
specters.

A man of humble origins, Heiss
wasn't born in a manger, but close
to it—Jersey City. His father was a
touring musician who played tenor
saxophone with Louis Armstrong.
His mother was a table-tipping
medium. In a letter to a childhood
friend, Heiss recounted the painful experience of learning that his
mother was a fraud, and that his

FIGURE 7.2.
Vernon Heiss

father only knew how to play three notes on the sax. Apparently Louis
Armstrong had a large band, and it was easy to get lost in the mix.

Disillusioned, young Vernon Heiss left home at the age of nine for the
mean streets of New York. (That may seem young, but back then it was
practically middle-aged.) He made money the only way he could: by hustling, first as a fortune-teller on the streets of Harlem, and later selling hast-
ily written and copied pamphlets promising to impart secrets of the sax. He
didn't make much money, but he made enough to get by. By the time he was
eighteen, he thought he'd seen everything there was to see in life.

That's when he saw his father's ghost.

Heiss hadn't even been aware his father had died until his ghost visited
him one cold December night in 1925. The ghost warned him that if he
didn't change his hustling ways, he would wind up alongside him in the
hellish spirit world.

Trembling, Vernon Heiss vowed to change.

He learned how to play his father's old sax, which had been left to him
in the will. And instead of writing misleading saxophone-lesson pamphlets,
he turned his pen to the paranormal. He joined the American Society for

Psychical Research and dove into their extensive case files and paranormal library, which the organization still maintains in Manhattan. (It's open to qualified scholars via appointment only. We haven't checked it out, but that's only because neither of us can afford to visit New York.)

In 1928, Heiss published *The Heiss Guide to Frightful Entities*, featuring his now legendary Occult Manifestation Index. Heiss separated paranormal entities by their general threat level, starting with the lowest levels of malevolence and increasing by manifolds of ten until reaching the "purest" evil beings. He organized them into three major "arcana"—a term borrowed from the tarot card system, showing he couldn't quite shake his mother's fortune-telling days after all—each of which contain three minor arcana. Of particular note is his inclusion of cats as "potentially dangerous" occult beings, which he believed was due to their use as witches' familiars. Pretty freaking weird, huh?

HEISS'S OCCULT MANIFESTATION INDEX

Major Arcana the First: Benign

Minor Arcana I—Common Haunting—Harmless, unseen specter.

Minor Arcana II—Ghoulie—Rarely visible (although sometimes irritating) wraith.

Minor Arcana III—Boggart—Mischievous household spirit; more annoying than dangerous. Partial-bodied apparition.

Major Arcana the Second: Potentially Dangerous

Minor Arcana IV—Fantasm—Full-bodied apparition. Non-humanoid.

Minor Arcana V—Cats—Cats.

Minor Arcana VI—Corporeal Entity—Full-bodied humanoid apparition. Offensive in both behavior and appearance.

Major Arcana the Third: Malevolent

Minor Arcana VII—Shkreli—Gaseous, mist-like apparition.

Minor Arcana VIII—Poltergeist—Violent, troublesome spirit.

Minor Arcana IX—Demon—Pure evil.

Source: Vernon Heiss. The Heiss Guide to Frightful Entities. *New York: Macmillan Publishers, 1928.*

Despite how foreign his system appears today, you'd be hard-pressed to find anyone in the field of parapsychology whose theories about spirits weren't somewhat influenced by Heiss. Unfortunately for Heiss, he wasn't around to reap the rewards of his success. *The Heiss Guide to Frightful Entities* was long out of print by the time he went missing while climbing Mt. Hood in 1932. His posthumous follow-up, *The Heiss Guide to Frightful Funguses*, bypassed bookstores and was sold to farmers as cattle feed (the unfortunate fate of many books during the Great Depression).

And if Vernon's surname sounds familiar, you're right: His grandson, Martin Heiss, is now a famous debunker of the paranormal. Kind of a pompous jerk about it, too.

Maureen Kemp's Spectral Field Guide

The most up-to-date and generally accepted taxonomy comes to us from Dr. Maureen Kemp (Figure 7.3), the paranormal scholar who took Vernon Heiss's work to the next level.

Following the end of World War II, Maureen Kemp's parents emigrated from Scotland to Chicago, where they raised their only child in a posh two-story manor on the North Side. Today, Kemp maintains a vivid recollection of her childhood in the evocative, almost gothic residence.

"Up until preschool, my nana used to bounce me on her knees for hours," she told *Newsweek* last year. "It was actually quite painful, because she had bony knees as if she were no more than a skeleton." Her grandmother would regale her with stories of back home in Scotland. Kemp's favorite stories were about the legendary sea serpent said to live in Loch Ness.

Kemp's parents were as down-to-earth as they come—real Midwesterners, who'd taken to their adopted homeland. They'd discarded the mystical ways of the old country. So when their otherwise intelligent four-year-old daugh-

FIGURE 7.3.
Maureen Kemp

ter casually mentioned the Loch Ness monster one afternoon, they asked where she'd heard such nonsense.

"From Nana," the child replied.

Her mother scoffed. "Tell us the truth, child. Where d'ya learn about Nessie?"

"I already told you," Kemp said. "From Nana."

Her parents exchanged troubled glances. "That's impossible," her father said. "Both of your grandmothers are dead. We put 'em in the same pine box, sixteen years past."

"'Twas to save on burial costs," her mother added, glancing nervously away. "We weren't so well off in those days. We never should have done it, but we did. If we could apologize, we'd do it in a heartbeat."

"But if she's dead . . ."

Kemp didn't have to complete the sentence. She'd been speaking to a ghost—she knew it. Her parents didn't believe her, though, and they chastised her for making up stories. (At least they didn't put her in therapy.) The old woman never materialized again. Perhaps the apology for her improper burial was all she'd been sticking around for; perhaps her time was simply up. Perhaps she had sinister intentions, but wasn't able to act on them now that Kemp's parents were wise to her. Who is to say?

While Kemp believed she'd been conversing with a ghost, she had doubts about her grandmother's stories about Nessie. The likelihood of a single, long-extinct plesiosaur roaming the waters of a small lake in the Scottish Highlands was remote. It was more plausible that her nana had seen a school of fish, or an eel, or perhaps the surfacing trunk of a bathing elephant.

It was exactly this same level of scientific reason and inquiry that Maureen Kemp would bring to the paranormal some years later. While Kemp was completing her doctoral work in psychology, a colleague turned her on to a fringe branch of academia: parapsychology. "I hadn't thought such a thing existed," she wrote in her autobiography, *Never Lonely: A Life Amongst the Spirits*. "Suddenly, my whole worldview transmogrified. Studying the living is so drab compared to studying the dead."

Her parents weren't happy with her change of career, but Kemp knew she had to follow her heart. The study of the paranormal isn't just a career; it's a calling. You don't stumble backwards into it. You charge headfirst—as fast as you can—until you make it. Kemp made few friends along the way, but made a name for herself with diligent research and impregnable results.

After earning her Ph.D. in parapsychology from the now-defunct program at the University of Northeastern California, Kemp began her ambitious life's work: *Kemp's Spectral Field Guide*, a comprehensive taxonomy of specters for the modern world.

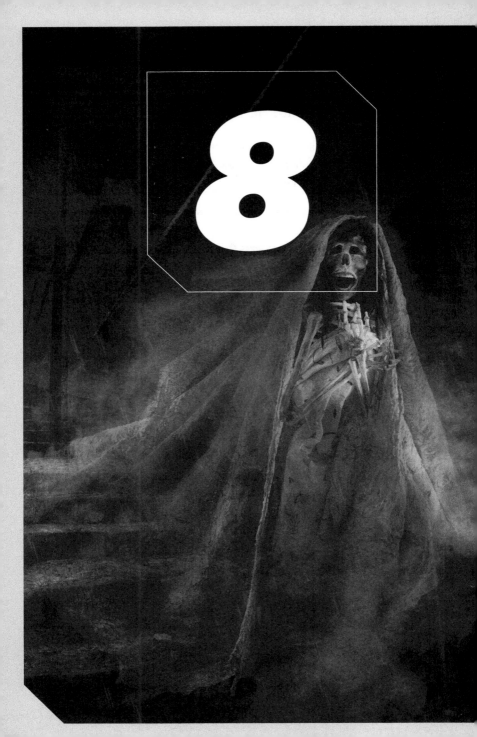

8

Vengeful Spirits and the Dangers of Their Return to Our World

Case Studies of Malevolent Entities

UBLISHED IN 1984, KEMP'S SPECTRAL FIELD GUIDE coincided with a brief resurgence of ghosts in popular entertainment. Michael Jackson's "Thriller" video was in constant rotation on MTV, and a bevy of paranormal-themed movies debuted that summer. Kemp's book rode the temporary supernatural wave and became an immediate sensation both with the public and with discerning paranormal investigators.

Today, it is widely acknowledged as the most accurate taxonomy of paranormal entities, spanning in Heiss-like fashion from the lowest levels of malevolence (Class I) to the highest (Class VII). So, without further ado . . .

Okay, Erin wants one last "ado." So there it is.

Good?

Yes, thank you.

Now let's move on!

Class I

What Kemp says: "Undeveloped ghosts with indefinite form. Includes partial ectoplasmic manifestations such as vapors and mists, as well as other sensory stimuli (disembodied voices, enigmatic knocking sounds, spectral orbs, etc.). Ability to physically manipulate objects in this world is extremely limited. Non-sentient. Usually harmless due to their physical insubstantiality."

FIGURE 8.1.
Class I: Will-o'-the-wisp

What we say: Until an ectoplasmic manifestation occurs or sentience is somehow detected, hauntings are generally considered Class I until proven otherwise. True Class I ghosts are difficult to verify at times. Unless somebody sees a vapor, mist, or spectral light, a random knocking noise could be anything, from mice in the walls to water pipes (or—ewwwww—mice in the water pipes).

CASE STUDIES

Will-o'-the-wisp: According to Peter Haining, author of *A Dictionary of Ghosts*, there's a long history of will-o'-the-wisps (Figure 8.1) throughout the United Kingdom and Europe. These spectral lights appear primarily in swamps and marshes as glowing white or blue orbs. They have been known to take on a more flame-like quality and glow red, orange, or yellow, as was the case for one Blaydon gentleman on a fox hunt in the spring of 1987. After seeing several of the spectral lights about a hundred yards into the woods, the man gave chase. Unfortunately, following a will-o'-the-wisp is a foolish proposition—no matter how long you run after the specter, the "foolish fire" remains just out of reach, as he learned.

FIGURE 8.2.
Class I: Ghostly Mist

Ghostly Mist: Ghostly mists (Figure 8.2) are vaporous states of ectoplasm that often precede further materializations, but sometimes appear and disappear on their own. Vernon Heiss tells the tale of a prototypical Class I mist in *The Heiss Guide to Frightful Entities*, wherein a concentrated, luminescent fog rolls across an Iowa cornfield and passes right through a transfixed farmer.

Direct Voice Phenomena (DVP): When Rhonda Kazdin heard the whispering children's voices in her attic, she did what any of us would do: SHE CALLED THE COPS. She assumed some neighborhood rapscallions had broken into her house. The policeman who arrived heard the whispers too, but discovered the attic was empty. What they heard was likely direct voice phenomena—disembodied spectral voices (Figure 8.3). Not all DVP is considered Class I. Evidence of sentience usually means some form of unseen ectoplasmic manifestation is either nearby or eminent, which would require reclassification. True Class I vocal-

FIGURE 8.3.
Class I: Direct Voice Phenomena (DVP)

izations may still include speech, snippets of songs, or, if you're particularly unlucky, slam poetry.

Class II

What Kemp says: "Ghosts with partial human form or behavior. Examples include spectral hands, animated lips, and other substantial physical compositions created out of ectoplasm by spirits. Unlike Class I entities, Class II entities are capable of physically manipulating objects, including levitating tables, chairs, and bedsheets, occasionally in the absence of visible ectoplasmic manifestations. Sentient, but lacking the willpower and strength to do major physical damage."

What we say: Most entities of this type appear to be a "bridge" between specters of the first and third classes. For instance, entities may appear first as a vaporous mist, before gaining the strength in this world to slowly take shape as a Class II manifestation and finally as a fully humanoid Class III ghost. Then again, there are still plenty of reports of ghosts that never progress past this stage. To which we say, don't worry. Difficulty manifesting completely is nothing to be ashamed of. It happens to plenty of ghosts.

FIGURE 8.4.
Class II: Disembodied Hand

CASE STUDIES

Disembodied Hand: A disembodied hand (Figure 8.4) makes a frightful appearance in the story of a house haunted by a Class II apparition in Joseph Glanvill's *Saducismus Triumphatus,* first published in 1681. Following several days of knocking noises and flying furniture, a spectral hand materialized—swinging a hammer. The hand chased the homeowners and disappeared, taking the hammer with it! Class II hauntings are among the most disturbing for parapercipients. Spectral lights and full-bodied ghosts are one thing; floating, disembodied hands are quite another. Some paranormal experiences are just too bewildering for our brains to comprehend. Unless, of course, they're within the context of a network sitcom. Looking at you, Thing.

Animated Lips: Ectoplasmic lips (Figure 8.5) and vocal cords may actually be behind many reports of Class II DVP. Animated lips are also capable of doing . . . other things. Ahem. Case studies are a little too graphic to include here, but we'll point you in the direction of Eleanor

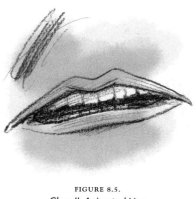

FIGURE 8.5.
Class II: Animated Lips

Fisk's *Fiends with Benefits: True Stories of Paranormal Love* for further reading.

Tipping Table: Tipping tables (Figure 8.6) were often reported during spiritualist séances. Occasionally, tables were even said to levitate—a frequent occurrence at séances conducted by Eusapia Palladino, the medium investigated by the Curies. Paranormal investigators and skeptics alike have panned the phenomenon of table tipping, believing its seemingly supernatural effects to be the result of subconscious muscle movements (similar to what happens when planchettes zip around Ouija boards). In some cases, table tipping may be the result of the intervention of Class II specters. In most, however, it is just a cheap trick—blatant manipulation by unscrupulous mediums and con people. Table tipping shouldn't be confused with table dancing, which is something else entirely (and not paranormal, unless the dancer is Class III or IV).

FIGURE 8.6.
Class II: Tipping Table

Class III

What Kemp says: "Ectoplasmic manifestations with distinct human form or behavior. Former identity not established. Significantly more developed than Class II entities, though may be missing body parts (legs, arms, head, etc.). Once a spirit's mortal progenitor has been positively established, it is automatically reclassified as Class IV."

What we say: Unlike Class I and II entities, Class IIIs are fully formed manifestations. The defining feature is (usually) a humanoid torso. Most have heads as well, although in some cases the head will be detached from the body and carried by the ghost (or simply missing). Other append-ages may be missing as well, al-though this is usually for purposes of expedience rather than a failure to fully manifest—it's just more fea-sible to float around without legs (even if those ectoplasmic legs aren't 100 percent solid-state). Possessions also fall under this class. Importantly, once the former identity of a Class III entity has been identified, it is reclas-sified as a Class IV entity.

FIGURE 8.7.
Class III: The Night Man

CASE STUDIES

The Night Man: The mildly annoying Night Man (Figure 8.7) is the ghost of an anonymous sailor who perished in a shipwreck off the coast of the Isle of Man. According to folklorist Dora Broome, this "strange and name-less figure" is often seen watching the clouds, and will toot his bugle when a storm is on the way. Perhaps he provided townspeople with a useful service back in the day, but we have meteorologists now, Mr. Night Man. Time to hang up the horn.

FIGURE 8.8.
Class III: Byron's Monk

Byron's Monk: Poet and gadfly Lord Byron once saw the full-figured ghost of an unknown monk at Newstead Abbey (Figure 8.8), inspiring him to write this little ditty: "A monk arrayed/ In cowl,

FIGURE 8.9.
Class III: The Blue Man

and beads, and dusky garb appeared,/ Now in the moonlight, and now lapsed in shade,/ With steps that trod as heavy, yet unheard." It doesn't *quite* rhyme, but we'll let that slide. Byron fired his pistol at the apparition, which he feared had come to claim his soul. The bullet went straight through the monk's ghostly figure and shattered a skull the poet often used as a wine goblet.

The Blue Man: Unrelated to the Blue Man Group, although both can make quite the racket. This full-bodied humanoid apparition haunts the twelfth-century Arundel Castle in Sussex, England. The Blue Man (Figure 8.9) is said to be that of an anonymous man in a blue silk suit—a dandy, in British parlance. Attempts to uncover the apparition's former identity have failed. While the Class III entity might dress impeccably, it is incredibly destructive and has no respect for personal space.

Class IV

What Kemp says: "Ectoplasmic manifestations with distinct human form or behavior. Similar to Class III ghosts, except the former identity of the spirit has been positively established."

What we say: Class III and IV ghosts are closely aligned with one another. In fact, the only differing characteristic is that Class IIIs are considered "anonymous hauntings," while Class IVs are positively identified as spirits of specific previously living beings. At first glance, this may seem like a quirk of Kemp's classification system, but trust us—it's like calling a spirit from the Minor Leagues up to the Majors. For ghost hunters who provide banishment or removal services, determining the mortal progenitor of a ghost is invaluable in choosing the best approach to resolving a haunting.

FIGURE 8.10.
Class IV: Arthur Conan Doyle

CASE STUDIES

Arthur Conan Doyle: Just minutes after Doyle's death, his spirit allegedly alerted his daughter that he had died. Mary Conan Doyle was at her father's library when a blank look came over the cleaning woman's face. The woman, in a trancelike state, announced that she was possessed by Doyle's ghost (Figure 8.10). He was using the woman to pass along news of his death—certainly not the conventional means of passing along such a notice, but one perfectly in line with Doyle's spiritualist beliefs. Not really malevolent behavior, unless you consider the traumatized cleaning woman who couldn't set foot in the Doyle household again.

FIGURE 8.11.
Class IV: John Belushi

John Belushi: The *Blues Brothers* star's mischievous ghost is said to haunt the Chateau Marmont in Hollywood, where he passed away at the age of thirty-three. According to an anonymous thread on the World Wide Web, a family staying in Belushi's former bungalow reportedly found their two-year-old son giggling to himself in the middle of the night. They asked him what was so hilarious. "The funny man," he said, much to their bewilderment. Years later, the grown child identified John Belushi (Figure 8.11) as the Class IV specter that had entertained him throughout the night.

Abraham Lincoln: A president's work is never done. The ghost of Abraham Lincoln (Figure 8.12) has appeared with such frequency at the White House that it's come to be known as "the White House Ghost." Teddy Roosevelt is among the many who have seen the Class IV entity: "I think of Lincoln, shambling, homely, with his sad, strong deeply furrowed face all the time. I see him in the different rooms and halls." Lincoln's ghost has also assumed control of mediums such as Leonora Piper and manifested in multiple locations (including Ford's Theatre), indicating the specter is of the free-roaming variety.

Class V

What Kemp says: "Ectoplasmic manifestations with definite, non-human form. Thought to be composites of residual PKE, these entities have no recognizable connection to their former lives in physical shape, thought, or behavior."

FIGURE 8.12.
Class IV: Abraham Lincoln

FIGURE 8.13.
Class V: The Zugspitze Terror

What we say: Class V entities are fully formed, but, unlike Class IIIs and IVs, the form is distinctly non-humanoid and tends to be more violent and powerful. Investigations into the history of a haunted locale with a Class V specter may reveal a multitude of sudden, violent deaths, which have led to a build-up of residual spirit energy. Battlefields and sites of natural disasters are common sites for Class V hauntings. Class V entities may also be the result of ritual summonings or other human meddling with the barrier.

CASE STUDIES

The Zugspitze Terror: Accompanied by a small army of reporters and photographers, ghost hunter Alexander St. Pierre marched to the top of

Germany's highest mountain peak at midnight on July 6, 1908, with a goat and a bag of chalk. He planned to perform a ritual summoning from *The Big Book of Blasphemy* that would turn the goat into a young maiden. Inside a magic circle drawn with chalk, St. Pierre read the incantation aloud. The resulting manifestation ripped everyone to shreds, including the poor, innocent goat. A dying victim's description of the Zugspitze Terror (Figure 8.13) is all that remains.

FIGURE 8.14.
Class V: The Hastings Fountain

The Hastings Fountain: A spectral fountain of blood (Figure 8.14) thought to be a residual composite has been seen northwest of Hastings in Sussex, England. Those who get too close to it are liable to be drowned by its overflowing ectoplasmic "waters." Paranormal historians believe the fountain represents the mass amounts of blood spilled on the battlefield where William the Conqueror fought the Anglo-Saxons in 1066, a battle that resulted in 15,000 to 20,000 dead.

FIGURE 8.15.
Class V: Mr. Skeltal

Mr. Skeltal: This ghost first appeared to visitors at National Battlefield Park in Richmond, Virginia, in 1973. Experts have speculated that the so-called "trumpet skeleton of the abyss" is composed of the residual spirit energy of Union trumpeters killed during the American Civil War. Mr. Skeltal (Figure 8.15) has since been seen around the world, playing the Civil War–era tune, "Weeping Sad and Lonely." The tune is said to drive parapercipients to madness.

Class VI

What Kemp says: "Ectoplasmic manifestations from the spirits of non-human terrestrial, extra-terrestrial, and lesser interdimensional life forms; most commonly animals or animalistic entities."

What we say: Ectoplasmic manifestations of any former living creature, excluding the spirits of human beings. Interdimensional entities that lack the godlike powers of metaspecters are also included in this category due to their base, animalistic behavior. Collectively, Class VI non-human entities are sometimes referred to as "elementals." Appearances can be deceiving. While the concept of a spectral cow seems absurd, trust us—it's not, if you're being chased by one! What Class VI specters lack in intelligence, they make up for with a greater capacity for malevolence.

CASE STUDIES

Kelpies: These shape-shifting horse ghosts are particularly malevolent spirits, according to Peter Haining. Kelpies (Figure 8.16) are notorious in their native Scotland for attempting to lure people to their deaths by offering free rides on their backs across rivers, only to dump their passengers midway across turbulent waters. While you may be asking what kind of blockhead hops on the back of a ghost horse in the first place, these manifestations are so dense that they're virtually indistinguishable from living horses (so cut the dozens of poor souls documented in *Celtic Magazine*'s "Tales of the Water-Kelpie" some slack).

FIGURE 8.16.
Class VI: Kelpie

Chagrin: Throughout Eastern European folklore you will find mention of chagrins, the ghosts of yellow hedgehogs (Figure 8.17). They are thought to mostly bother horses, although they have been known to annoy humans from time to time. Their main method of attack is a stream of ectoplasmic urine, sprayed on victims. The "devil's baptism" is said to invariably cause misfortune or prognosticate misfortune. Either way, you've been used as a toilet by the ghost of a hedgehog—a misfortune in and of itself. We won't mention any parapercipients who have reported being victimized by chagrins, for obvious reasons.

FIGURE 8.17.
Class VI: Chagrin

Derwyn Corph: According to *A Dictionary of Ghosts,* the derwyn corph (Figure 8.18) is a Welsh spirit said to appear on the windowsill and repeatedly tap on the window, indicating the room's occupant will soon pass away. A derwyn corph was once spotted in Appalachia by the nurse in a hospice ward, tapping up a storm outside of several patients' windows. You can guess what happened next, but did the birds really have to be such annoying d-bags about it? Talk about malevolence.

Class VII

What Kemp says: "Metaspecters. Very powerful interdimensional entities with god-like powers. Capable of assuming multiple forms through the manipulation of ectoplasm, thus making them difficult to categorize without a fully detailed workup."

FIGURE 8.18.
Class VI: Derwyn Corph

What we say: These are the big girls and boys. You might know them as deities or demons; you might even recognize some of their names, such as Cthulhu. Ancient cultures have, at times, worshipped them as gods and

FIGURE 8.19.
Class VII: Cthulhu

goddesses. We don't know if we'd go that far down the supreme being route, but they're certainly god-*like*.

CASE STUDIES

Cthulhu: While many believe this cosmic deity was created by horror writer H. P. Lovecraft in the 1920s, descriptions of the gigantic, winged metaspecter (Figure 8.19) date back to the Protodynastic period. The deity's original Babylonian name, "Cathulhu," translates as "High Priest of the Great Old Ones." The physical manifestation of Cthulhu is said to stand dozens of stories tall. If the tales told about him are true, he has laid waste to numerous civilizations using nothing more than his bare hands. Modern-day Cthulhu cultists await the High Priest's re-emergence from his underwater hibernation.

FIGURE 8.20.
Class VII: Āpshai

Āpshai: According to the Egyptian *Book of the Dead*, Āpshai (Figure 8.20) is the evil Egyptian God of Insects. Āpshai is one of a pantheon of dark forces capable of obscuring the light of the sun god, Rā. Āpshai has been depicted as taking the shape of numerous insects, including the Egyptian pygmy mantis and the scarab. Regardless of what physical manifestation the entity takes, Āpshai is capable of summoning and controlling hordes of insects to cause pestilence—enough to literally black out the sun.

FIGURE 8.21.
Class VII: Krampus

Krampus: This horned, cloven-footed demon's origins can be traced back to pre-Christian pagan mythology. Krampus (Figure 8.21) is said to punish naughty children at Christmastime by swatting them with bundles of birch. Particularly deviant children may be kidnapped and taken to the underworld, to be cooked and eaten. Don't worry too much, parents: Although it is theoretically possible for an entity to abscond into another dimension with a sack full of kidnapped children, it's more likely he fries them up on this side of the barrier.

Addendum

Within each class, entities can be further described using various paranormal properties. For instance, a "Class V free-roaming vapor" is a Class V entity with a gaseous appearance not anchored to a fixed location. The ghost of Gretta DeMille, seen by Erin when she was eight, would be considered a Class IV anchored free-floating full-torso partially repeating apparition. Try saying *that* five times fast.

PARANORMAL PROPERTIES

- **Anchored:** Fixed to a specific location. Most long-term hauntings are the result of anchored entities.
- **Animating:** Capable of animating an object, either through telekinesis or para-transferral embodiment. For entities permanently bound to inanimate objects, see *Inhabiting*.
- **Composite:** Consisting of multiple, interconnected entities.
- **Corporeal:** Tangible; having physical form. Corporeal entities can be ranked on a five-point physical interactivity scale, from T1 (lowest) to T5 (highest).
- **Ethereal:** Intangible; without physical form.
- **Floating:** Maneuvers around at will, with little to no regard for the natural laws of our world. If a floating entity can move through walls, people, and other physical objects, it is considered "free-floating."
- **Focused:** See *Anchored*.
- **Free-floating:** See *Floating*.
- **Free-roaming:** Not anchored to any specific location.
- **Full-torso:** Entities complete with upper and lower bodies. Extremely rare. See also *Partial-torso*.

- **Grounded:** Moves according to natural laws (i.e., unable to levitate). See also *Floating*.
- **Inhabiting:** Permanently bound to an inanimate object. For temporary possessions or animations, see *Animating*.
- **Partial-torso:** Entities without full bodies. Generally missing legs, arms, or both. See also *Full-torso*.
- **Possessing:** Spectral possession of living beings or inanimate objects via para-transferral embodiment. For permanent possession of inanimate objects, see *Inhabiting*.
- **Repeating:** Manifests at intervals. Typically anchored. May be "reliving" its final moments on Earth or performing some other task, with or without regard to being watched by observers.
- **Transmogritive:** Able to shape-shift at will.
- **Vaporous:** Gaseous, misty, or otherwise wholly or partially insubstantial.

We have no idea how closely real ghosts match the descriptions found in *Kemp's Spectral Field Guide*. Her classification system is based on centuries of ghost stories and parapercipient reports, painstakingly organized into a speculative taxonomy. It's possible one or more of her classifications don't have a real-world equivalent. For instance, Class VII entities may not even exist. We know that could be heartbreaking for those of you hoping to cuddle a spectral sloth! Take solace in the fact that, if such an entity does exist, the last thing you would want to do is get close enough to pet it. First, you'd end up with ghost slime all over your hands. And second, it would probably tear your throat out. But we digress.

If we're ever going to truly further our understanding of the paranormal, we will need to leave theories and taxonomies behind and head into the field. In the next section, we'll do just that. Let the ghost hunting begin!

Our Methods

PART 3—AT A GLANCE

THIS IS IT: THE METAPHYSICAL EXAMINATION. SO HOW DOES a "ghost hunt" work, you ask? Don't worry—revealing one's methods is an important part of any serious study, and we're going to walk you through ours step-by-step, just like the New Kids.

The first methodical guide to paranormal investigation was written by Harry Price in 1937. He issued the short, eight-page pamphlet of instructions to volunteers who assisted him with his stakeout of the Borley Rectory. Since that time, many ghost hunters have come and gone, each adding to the collective body of knowledge. Every successive generation builds upon the work of previous generations. In this sense, we're just standing on the shoulders of the giants who came before us. We're like the cheerleaders at the top of the pyramid, except we're not showing off our underwear.

In **Chapter 9**, we're going to cover the tools of the paranormal trade every investigator needs before embarking into the unknown—and we'll let you know what you can leave behind. In **Chapter 10**, we'll walk you through finding a haunted location. In **Chapter 11**, we'll explain how to undertake the metaphysical examination and what to do if you encounter a spectral presence. And, finally, in **Chapter 12**—just in case your paranormal hotline isn't ringing off the hook—you'll learn how to lure spirits into our world . . . and why it's important that you never undertake such a task, except in the most controlled of circumstances.

CHAPTER 9

Paratechnology: A Primer

THERE HAS NEVER BEEN A BETTER TIME TO BE A PARA-normal investigator. Today's paratechnology is the most advanced we've ever seen. In fact, some of the tools available are so advanced, they are outpacing our knowledge of how to use them.

Paratechnology includes any technology used to observe or effect paranormal activity. Among the traditional tools are such mainstays as cameras and flashlights. More recent innovations such as ion detectors often cost hundreds or thousands of dollars. In fact, paratechnology, once the domain of do-it-yourself hobbyists, is now big business.

The sad truth, though, is that we're probably still years away from scientifically sound ghost-detecting technology, especially of the handheld variety, within reach of your average paranormal investigator. We'll go through every one of these gadgets one by one, but be forewarned: Not even the most expensive gadget on the market today can detect spectral particles. Most paratechnology works by detecting transmogrifications in the physical world thought to be associated with materializations, such as ionization of the air and electromagnetic fluctuations.

Unfortunately, plenty of "real world" phenomena can also cause false positives. For instance, many investigators utilize thermometers to detect sudden changes in air temperature—fluctuations thought to be related to psychical manifestations. Know what else is associated with a rapid change in temperature? A draft from an open door or window! Controlling all of the various physical variables in the field—more often than not an old house creakier than your grandma's knees—is next to impossible. Not that it can't be done, but even a positive ID of a Class VII using every tool in this chapter isn't going to stand up in the scientific courtroom.

Still, that's no reason not to do fieldwork. It's difficult enough to get someone to open their door and let you in to investigate, so you'd better come prepared to do a bang-up job. With that said, let's take a look at the tools essential for conducting metaphysical examinations, as well as the ones serious ghost hunters have deemed nonessential.

Animals: Unless you're an old pro at this ghost-hunting business, you may be scratching your head, going "Huh?" Let us enlighten you: *Some experts actually advise the use of companion animals during paranormal investigations.* Certain animals, such as dogs and horses, are thought to have the ability to sense paranormal entities. They're often restless or agitated just prior to the appearance of ghosts, although such data is purely anecdotal. In addition to dogs and horses, some parapsychologists believe that cats also possess this "sixth sense." While cats have been observed meowing uncontrollably or acting stir-crazy in haunted areas, that could just be cats being cats. Before bringing pets along on a stakeout, further study must be done to determine why certain animal species appear to have forewarning of ectoplasmic manifestations while others—including human beings—must rely on more ordinary-seeming senses.

FIGURE 9.1.
Cassette Tape

Audio Recorder: While working in his darkroom in 1936, artist Attila von Szalay heard the voice of his dead brother call out to him. Convinced of the reality of the afterlife, he made several attempts over the years to record spirit voices. Using a reel-to-reel tape recorder, von Szalay finally recorded the disembodied voices of what he believed to be spirits in the summer of 1956. Despite not hearing anything while recording, the voices on his tape said . . . um, "Hot dog, Art!" and "Merry Christmas and Happy New Year to you all." Not exactly Earth-shattering communications, and a reminder that not every ghost that returns through the barrier is seeking vengeance. Sometimes they just want to wish us a Merry Christmas. In July.

As you learned in Chapter 3, such recordings fall under the heading of electronic voice phenomena (EVP). EVP is usually picked up on magnetic tape (Figure 9.1), and heard only upon playback. Critics say this is because what we call "EVP" is nothing more than electromagnetic interference. As proof, they point to digital recorders, which do not pick up nearly as much EVP as analog devices.

Despite the controversy surrounding EVP, we advise carrying an audio recorder. We recommend digital over tape if you can afford it, as there's less risk of electromagnetic interference tainting the results. We've also read promising things about using three or more units spaced out equidistant from a central point, which allows sound sources to be triangulated. As a bonus, you can also use your audio recorder for interviewing witnesses. Or recording yourself singing your favorite pop songs, if you're too cheap to buy the CDs, like Erin.

FIGURE 9.2.
Natural Enemy of the Ghost Hunter

Batteries: Always carry spares. The most common battery sizes are AA, AAA, and 9-volt, but it's best just to carry a wide assortment. Even if none of your gear requires D batteries, they're hefty and good for plunking raccoons that get all up in your business. Yes, you heard that correctly—raccoons (Figure 9.2).

We don't want to run afoul of PETA here, but as paranormal investigators we have a right to defend ourselves when attacked by wild animals in the field. These fat trash-hamsters like to creep around haunted houses. Be careful in attics, basements, and other dimly lit areas. If a raccoon isn't scared away when plunked with a D battery, it means either the raccoon has rabies and isn't frightened of anything—RUN!—or the creature is actually a Class VI specter in the shape of a raccoon. In that case, snap a quick picture or two and *then* run.

Blacklight: These UVA lights are useful for illuminating rooms to check for traces of ectoplasm, which is thought to glow a bright white under long-wave ultraviolet light. You don't need one of the big tubes found at Spencer's; a small handheld unit should suffice. You're ghost hunting, not hosting a rave in your dorm room.

Camera: Cameras are among the most popular items for ghost hunters. While we can't trap a ghost with current paratechnology, we can catch a ghost on film. JUST CHECK OUT ALL THE ORB PHOTOS WE TOOK!!! In addition to still photography, video cameras are also used by many paranormal investigators. Night-vision and thermographic filters (including heat graphs, like the one Predator uses!) are available for both still and video cameras. We suggest using the best camera you can afford.

Carbon Monoxide Detector: There is growing evidence that carbon-monoxide poisoning might be responsible for some "ghost sightings." While the colorless, odorless gas eventually kills its victims, it also causes confusion, nausea, and hallucinations—all symptoms that may be incorrectly interpreted by parapercipients as evidence of a spectral presence. One famous case of such an occurrence was published in the *American Journal of Ophthalmology*, of all places, in 1921. A patient of Dr. William Wilmer, identified only as "Mrs. H.," described her family's experience: The governess reported hearing footsteps when nobody was home, and the children grew listless and tired (clearly not the natural state for children). The chimney was found to be blocked, causing carbon monoxide to be drawn into the house instead of expelled. Once this was fixed, the "hauntings" ceased. Carrying your own carbon-monoxide detector isn't a bad idea, since many older homes may not have one installed.

Compass: Compasses were one of the earliest tools used by paranormal investigators to detect spectral entities. The needle on a compass always points north . . . unless there's spectral activity. When spirits are allegedly nearby, compasses have been known to spin wildly out of control. Of course, there may be mundane explanations for a confused compass, including interference from electromagnetic sources. Still, it can't hurt to pack one—in case you get lost in the woods investigating a haunting, a compass may just save your life by guiding you to safety. Unless it goes haywire due to paranormal phenomena, of course. Then you're screwed.

Dowsing Rod: Dowsing rods—also known as divining rods—have been used for hundreds of years to search for underground water, buried treasure, and practically anything else that can be hidden beneath the Earth, including human remains.

When the dowsing rod senses the object the user is seeking, it bends toward the ground or otherwise goes batty (much like a compass supposedly does in the presence of a ghost). Although they can be as simple as a branch or pendulum, the dowsing rods most commonly used by ghost hunters are L-shaped metal rods that come in pairs. DIY paranormal investigators often save themselves a few bucks by bending a couple of metal hangers.

Multiple studies have been commissioned to study the art of dowsing. The results have been disappointing, to say the least. You'd be better off hauling around a metal detector than a dowsing rod. It won't lead you to any ghosts, but you could wind up with enough spare change to buy yourself some new hangers that aren't bent to hell.

FIGURE 9.3.
EMF Meter

EMF Meter: Popularized by TV ghost hunters, these handheld devices (Figure 9.3) detect fluctuations in AC electromagnetic fields. The human body is known to produce low-level electromagnetic radiation in the form of brain waves—about 12 watts, at any given time. Do spectral entities produce similar radiation? Possibly. The problem, however, is that such a low level of radiation is virtually undetectable at short distances by even the most expensive EMF meters. Until the technology improves, you're more likely to detect a running refrigerator than a supernatural entity.

Flashlight: Ghost hunting in the dark without a flashlight or some other source of illumination is a foolhardy business. Every member of your team should carry a flashlight along with spare batteries. While we're on the topic, you do have a team, right? Ghost hunting isn't the sort of thing you want to be doing by your lonesome, as Abby's grandma would say. Know what else her grandma would say? *Wear a coat, because you'll catch a cold.* Abby would always put up a fight. The common cold is caused by a virus, not by cool temperatures. Her grandma would relent, and Abby would go without a coat to school, and three days later she would have a sore throat and runny nose. This didn't prove her grandma was right, however. All it proved is that schools are germ factories. What were we talking about? Anyway, take a flashlight.

Geiger Counter: Hans Holzer said it best: "Don't take any equipment with you like Geiger counters. It's all bull." If your handheld Geiger counter detects ionizing radiation such as alpha or beta particles, you've probably got bigger problems than ghosts to deal with. THESE ARE NOT THE IONS YOU'RE LOOKING FOR. This is probably a good time to let you know you shouldn't be ghost hunting inside nuclear power plants. While spirits do plague them— just like anywhere else—there are much safer places to conduct investigations.

Gun: Ghost hunter Elliott O'Donnell was known to barge into haunted houses, revolver at the ready. Fortunately, he never seriously injured himself or any homeowners during his investigations. It should go without saying that guns, crossbows, and other weapons would have only a limited impact on ectoplasm, and do nothing to disperse the PKE behind such manifestations. Leave them at home.

Infrasound Monitoring Equipment: The typical hearing range for the human ear is 20 to 20,000 Hz. While we have difficulty hearing other frequencies, there is plenty of evidence that we can sense them in other ways. "Infrasound" below the lower limits of our hearing capabilities has been known to cause feelings of dread and unpleasantness in test subjects, earning it the nickname "the fear frequency." Infrasound occurs naturally in the environment (e.g., thunder, wind, the roar of a tiger). One researcher re-

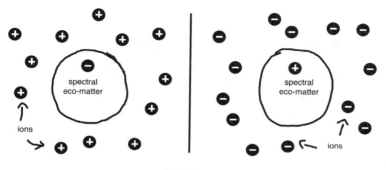

FIGURE 9.4.
Ionization of air, according to Spectral Field Theory:
By pulling electrons from surrounding atoms, negatively charged eco-matter causes an
excess of positive ions in the air (left). Positively charged spectral eco-matter loses electrons to
surrounding atoms, causing an excess of negative ions (right).
Abby, created in MS Paint

corded infrasound being issued from an extremely flatulent elephant! (From both ends!) Infrasound may also be generated by furnaces or other appliances in homes, leading some researchers to posit that infrasound contributes to the uneasiness felt by parapercipients at haunted locales. While it's still speculative, carrying infrasound monitoring equipment could be beneficial, especially in cases where Class I spirits have been reported.

Ion Detector: If our theory of spectral materialization is correct, an excess of ions (positive or negative, depending upon ethereal polarization) should be detectable when ghosts manifest. Ions are molecules that have gained or lost electrons (Figure 9.4). They are odorless and harmless. High-density ion concentrations occur in the environment without spectral particle agitation, so it is important to rule out natural explanations (such as thunderstorms) if excess ions are detected. Ion detectors are pricey, but worth the investment.

Motion Detector: Wireless motion sensors should be set up in rooms where ghosts may materialize. While Class I ghosts won't trigger a motion detector, physical manifestations (Class II or higher) might. They're cheaper than setting up video cameras, which will save you a lot of money since the typical haunted house has an average of thirteen rooms. Motion detectors can also alert you if a raccoon tries poking its snout around your investigation.

Night-Vision Goggles: Flashlights are nice for illuminating low-light conditions, but night-vision goggles are a thousand times better. They're also about a thousand times as expensive.

Notebook: Paper is one of mankind's oldest technologies, having been invented almost 2,000 years ago in China. Despite its age, paper remains one of the most important pieces of the ghost hunter's tool kit. Everything that happens during the course of a metaphysical examination must be recorded in meticulous detail, from paranormal phenomena to parapercipient interviews. Never leave home without a notebook and an ample supply of writing instruments.

Thermometer: If a thermographic camera is out of your price range, a simple indoor/outdoor thermometer can be used to record ambient temperature changes. As we've already pointed out, some researchers believe sudden shifts in temperature, much like changes in electromagnetic and magnetic fields, are associated with paranormal activity. Because many natural reasons exist for these fluctuations, we're skeptical. Now, if you can use a rectal thermometer to take a ghost's temperature, that would be proof. Of what, we're not sure. But proof nonetheless.

Toilet Paper: Not technically paratechnology, but it's better to be safe than sorry. And while we're at it, don't forget to pack an extra pair of underwear.

Walkie-Talkies: Handheld two-way radio transceivers—or "walkie-talkies"—are an essential tool for all ghost hunters. Since paranormal investigators should always conduct on-site investigations in teams of two or more, you need a way to stay in constant contact with one another. While two-way radios aren't your only option, they're the best one on the market. Cellular phones are large, bulky, and work poorly indoors; pagers are for drug dealers and philosophy majors. As a bonus, you never know when your two-way radio receiver will suddenly pick up spectral interference (i.e., radio voice phenomena).

Watch: Stylish. Versatile. Indispensable, as you'll need to note the exact time of paranormal occurrences in your notebook. And, if you get one like Erin's, it has a calculator built right into it! Then you can do calculations on the fly. Like calculating how much to leave as a tip at Denny's after a long night of ghost hunting.

The Ghostbusters' Arsenal: An Update

BY JILLIAN HOLTZMANN

Paratechnology has come a long way since the nineties. While you can still find would-be ghost hunters bumbling around in the dark with bent coat hangers—it's as easy as flipping on your TV and tuning in to whatever channel is desperate enough these days to air *Ghost Jumpers*—real parapsychologists have progressed beyond such toys. And for that, we have Drs. Yates and Gilbert to thank.

The Yates-Gilbert Equation, first proposed by Abby and Erin in the original edition of *Ghosts from Our Past,* laid the foundation for the paratechnological advances of the past two decades. While their theory has yet to achieve consensus from the scientific community, it continues to gain ground amongst forward-thinking physicists. More important, the Yates-Gilbert Equation provided the theoretical blueprints for the PKE-based tools that Abby and I developed during our time together at the Kenneth P. Higgins Institute of Science.

After we left the school and formed the Ghostbusters, the designs continued to evolve, especially after we were able to test out our equipment on actual ghosts. This cutting-edge paratechnology not only detects spectral particles, but it gives us the option of subduing and trapping ghosts for containment and further study—something Erin and Abby thought all but impossible back when they first wrote *Ghosts from Our Past.*

While I'm not able to share every detail about the paratechnology we utilize until the patents are finalized—the Ghostbusters are a commercial enterprise, after all—here's a quick look at some of the gear you may have seen us hauling around Midtown.

PKE Meter: PKE meters (Figure 9.5) are high-sensitivity ghost-tracking units used to detect the presence of spectral particles (i.e., psychokinetic energy). These handheld units can also be used to establish the nature of substances and objects believed to be of paranormal origin. PKE meters are equipped with a transducer that converts data into a visually accessible format displayed on the built-in display. Spectral masses appear as pinpoints on a sonar-style graphical interface, allowing for real-time tracking. As the user nears the source of the PKE, the spinning antennae separate and form a V-shape.

FIGURE 9.5.
PKE Meter

Proton Pack (Mark II): The proton pack (Figure 9.6) generates a beam of positively charged ions (or "proton stream") to counter ghosts' negatively charged energy. (In cases of positively charged ectoplasm, polarity can be reversed.) The proton pack is composed of two parts: a backpack housing a portable particle accelerator, and an attached handheld plasma thrower (or "wand"). At lower proton beam strength, the proton stream temporarily subdues ghosts by weakening their ectoplasmic bonds. This allows the user to hold the spectral manifestation in place long enough to deploy a ghost trap. Permanent dispatch of entities is possible at higher settings, although the proton stream's effects upon spectral energy vary greatly depending upon the ghost's class. Also, with great power comes great responsibility—I'm talking about property damage and the like. Lower beam current settings are therefore recommended for everyday use.

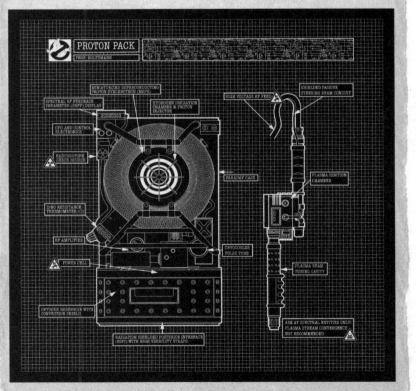

FIGURE 9.6.
Proton Pack and Wand (Mark II)

Compared to earlier versions of the proton pack, the Mark II is considerably more compact. Its operation has been streamlined quite a bit: Protons are produced from hydrogen plasma in the ionization chamber and injected by high-voltage electrodes into a miniaturized superconducting proton synchrotron (MSPS). Next, the super-conducting synchrotron (outfitted with liquid helium-cooled magnets) accelerates the protons, which are then fed to the wand via the shielded beam-steering conduit. The Faraday cage attenuates RF noise and provides physical protection to avoid quenches while the cryocooler counteracts helium boil-off from the cryogen reservoir to increase operational time.

The wand contains its own beam-position monitoring components and active-steering electronics. Although the plasma beam halo can be tuned using the embedded quadrupoles, the plasma discharge from the output beam's passage through the air causes strong distortion and defocusing. This can make the wand quite unwieldy at times, especially for the novice user. Don't skip upper-body days at the gym.

Alas, due to regulatory concerns, I probably shouldn't mention how the proton pack is powered . . . but let's just say that the battery has a half-life longer than americium-25. Or equal to americium-25. You know what? Let's just forget I said anything about americium-25.

PROTON PACK WARNINGS

- Never point the wand at a living person. Even in jest.
- Avoid wearing loose-fitting clothing during operation.
- Keep out of reach of children. Particle accelerators are not toys.
- Do not touch the wand's nozzle when hot.
- Exercise extreme caution when using indoors. And outdoors.
- Plasma stream convergence is highly, highly discouraged.

Ghost Trap: The ghost trap (Figure 9.7) has one job, but it's an important one: It traps paranormal pests long enough to transfer them into the ecto-containment system back at Ghostbusters headquarters.

Using a ghost trap is as easy as setting a mousetrap, really. First, spectral entities need to be coaxed into range with application of a proton beam. Once activated, the trap's doors are opened and the PKE "sink" engaged. Leveraging ethereal polarization, the PKE sink attracts spectral disturbances of a given polarization. Once a specter has been pulled into the trap, the shielded containment doors close. The chamber acts as an ethereal resonance cavity, trapping the entity between nodes of standing waves in the spectral field. Traps should

FIGURE 9.7.
Ghost Trap

ideally be used to house only a single entity at a time. An occupancy indicator lights up, letting the user know if someone—or something—is inside. And if the trap is a-rockin', don't come a-knockin'. Seriously: If it starts bouncing around, don't touch it. Or kiss it. Looking at you, Erin.

Jillian Holtzmann is a former associate professor of paranormal studies at the Kenneth P. Higgins Institute of Science. A brilliant nuclear engineer, she was once considered for a position at the European Organization for Nuclear Research. These days, you can find Holtzmann at the Ghostbusters' headquarters in New York City, where she is Senior Proton Wrangler. Actually, she doesn't have an official job title—none of the Ghostbusters do. Still, even a made-up title sounds better than just saying she "dicks around with ghostbusting equipment all day."

10

Preparing for the Metaphysical Examination
Choosing a Location

OW THAT YOU HAVE THE PROPER EQUIPMENT, the next step is finding a haunted location. In some respects, we are on the verge of a golden age of ghost hunting. As the World Wide Web continues to grow, news of paranormal incidents is spreading faster than ever. Unfortunately, as we've discussed, parapercipients are just as reticent as ever to let metaphysical examiners into their homes. Maybe more so.

One way to find agreeable parapercipients is to advertise. The Ghost Club, for instance, boldly announced their intentions in an ad in the *Daily Telegraph*, expressing their "desire to obtain a house haunted by ghosts, in town or in country, for a limited period." Subsequent groups, such as the Society for Psychical Research, attempted similar stunts, usually attracting their fair share of pranksters and unstable individuals. So this isn't the best route, really.

You may have better results by asking friends or family for referrals (provided they are sympathetic to your beliefs) or keeping an eye out for stories of strange occurrences in the local newspaper. You will obviously need to obtain the homeowner's approval to investigate the premises. Understandably, many owners of private residences aren't keen on having a group of ghost hunters camp out overnight, waving strange beeping devices and taking photographs.

Businesses are equally wary of ghost hunters—they don't want anyone disturbing their customers, after all. The good news is many businesses *will* open themselves up for investigation during off-hours, especially if a troublesome specter is bothering customers and staff. Just be forewarned that if the business advertises itself as haunted, it's probably already been investigated to death (no pun intended).

Here's a breakdown of the most commonly haunted types of locations, from haunted houses to paranormal penitentiaries.

Commonly Haunted Locations

Houses: Houses, without a doubt, are the most haunted of all locales. Not only do homes outnumber other structures, but they're where we spend the bulk of our time—eating, sleeping, and, yes, dying. The older the home, the more likely it is to be haunted, simply by virtue of the greater number of residents who've inhabited the structure. When you're looking for haunted houses, don't neglect apartment buildings, trailers, and other dwellings. Except for dorms. Dorms are haunted only by hairspray and bad decisions.

Examples of Haunted Houses: Aldridge Mansion (New York City, New York), Belcourt Castle (Newport, Rhode Island), Lemp Mansion (St. Louis, Missouri), Moore House (Villisca, Iowa), Myrtles Plantation (St. Francisville, Louisiana), The White House (Washington, D.C.), Winchester Mansion (San Jose, California)

Theaters: Virtually every historic theater or opera house has a resident ghost. These supernatural nuisances cause actors to stumble, lights to flicker, and props to falter during performances. Some people believe that audiences, musicians, and actors release emotional energy during performances, which encourages spectral activity. What's more likely is that when accidents happen on stage, it's easier to blame them on a spook rather than anyone involved in the production. Scout theaters with a healthy dose of skepticism.

Examples of Haunted Theaters: Bobby Mackey's Music World (Wilder, Kentucky), Lincoln Theater (Decatur, Illinois), Metropolitan Opera House (New York City, New York), Stonebrook Theatre (New York City, New York)

Inns and Hotels: All it takes is one suicide or murder for a hotel to pick up a reputation for being haunted. Unfortunately, most inns and hotels will exaggerate the degree to which they are haunted for publicity. And if they're boasting about it, the phenomena is most likely family-friendly—nothing too exciting is going to happen. The hot tub's never going to bubble red with blood. If you're interested in investigating a *real* haunted hotel, we suggest finding one where hotel management vigorously denies any paranormal activity.

Examples of Haunted Inns and Hotels: Castle Hill Inn (Newport, Rhode Island), Jerome Grand Hotel (Jerome, Arizona), The Mercado (New York City, New York), Silver Queen Hotel (Virginia City, Nevada), The Stanley Hotel (Estes Park, Colorado)

Battlefields: Because of the huge number of deaths occurring on battlefields, it makes sense from a statistics standpoint that at least some of the fallen would return as ghosts. Apparitions of soldiers are often seen repeating their final actions, over and over. Additionally, some experts believe that mass emotional trauma causes buildups of telekinetic energy at battlefields, which in turn triggers visual disturbances in the minds of parapercipients. Unlikely, but who knows?

Examples of Haunted Battlefields: The Alamo (San Antonio, Texas), Gettysburg (Gettysburg, Pennsylvania), National Battlefield Park (Richmond, Virginia)

Prisons: Neither of us has been to prison, so we can't tell you how haunted the vibes are in "the joint." Most facilities, however, have long histories of suicides, murders, and other atrocities. Paranormal incident reports occur at the highest rates in those former prisons where executions have taken place—it seems that some prisoners never get to leave, even after dying.

Examples of Haunted Prisons: Alcatraz (San Francisco, California), Eastern State Penitentiary (Philadelphia, Pennsylvania), West Georgia Correctional Facility (Newnan, Georgia)

Hospitals: Surprisingly, hospitals aren't particularly known for being overrun with ghosts. However, there are plenty of exceptions, especially in the cases of old, abandoned asylums such as the Waverly Hills Sanatorium in Louisville, Kentucky—a former tuberculosis clinic spooky enough even without any paranormal happenings.

Examples of Haunted Hospitals: Bellevue Hospital (New York City, New York), Danvers State Hospital (Danvers, Massachusetts), Metropolitan

State Hospital (Waltham, Massachusetts), Rolling Hills Asylum (Bethany, New York), Waverly Hills Sanitarium (Louisville, Kentucky)

Cemeteries: Final resting places such as graveyards aren't the best places to hunt ghosts. Nobody, not even ghosts, wants to hang out on such hallowed ground. While reportedly haunted graveyards do exist, we don't suggest ghost hunting at these locations. Respect the families of the deceased. Don't be a creeper.

Examples of Haunted Cemeteries: Bachelor's Grove Cemetery (Midlothian, Illinois), Boot Hill Cemetery (Tombstone, Arizona), Howard Street Cemetery (Salem, Massachusetts), St. Louis Cemetery No. 1 (New Orleans, Louisiana), Westminster Hall and Burying Ground (Baltimore, Maryland)

THE 13 MOST HAUNTED U.S. CITIES

- Baltimore, Maryland
- Boston, Massachusetts
- Charleston, South Carolina
- Chicago, Illinois
- Fort Lauderdale, Florida
- New Orleans, Louisiana
- New York City, New York
- Portland, Oregon
- Salem, Massachusetts
- San Antonio, Texas
- San Francisco, California
- Savannah, Georgia
- Washington, D.C.

None of which are in Michigan. Sigh.

Source: Josephine Bandette. The Occult Encyclopaedia: In Thirteen Volumes. *Cambridge, MA: Harvard University Press, 1919.*

Research the Location

Once you've settled on a location for your investigation, you'll want to do some serious research before ever setting foot on-site. Look up its history at the county assessor's office. Better yet, check with your local librarian to see if there's any documented history of paranormal activity associated with the site. Librarians love to do research. They shouldn't have any problem sifting through a hundred or so years of newspapers on microfiche to answer your query (allow four to six weeks for a thorough investigation, and don't forget to tip). In addition to a history of paranormal activity, you'll also want to know the history of the people who've lived and died at the site—and a detailed history of the land itself. Once you have that in hand, you're ready to begin the metaphysical examination!

Haunted History: Case Studies

BY PATTY TOLAN

As an NYC transit station agent, I had plenty of time to read. Especially on the overnight shift. Sure, every once in a while a subway rider would interrupt me, but I'd interrupt them right back. Hey, it's the Big Apple. I had my own one-person book club going for a long time in my little subway booth. This wasn't an Oprah deal—no Franzen or Tolstoy. I've always been more of a history buff. Here's a selection of haunted locations, prepared especially for the revised edition, courtesy of the extensive research unwittingly funded by the Metropolitan Transit Authority.

Aldridge Mansion (New York City, New York): This stately West Village brownstone (Figure 10.1) is the only nineteenth-century home in New York City "preserved both inside and out," according to the Aldridge Mansion Museum's website. While that sounds like some marketing nonsense, the story behind the building's haunting isn't: One morning, Sir Aldridge awoke furious when his breakfast wasn't waiting for him. He called out to his servants, but no one responded. Sir Aldridge found their lifeless bodies in their quarters. They'd been stabbed to death by his eldest daughter, Gertrude. To spare the family public humiliation, the embarrassed patriarch locked her in the basement, where he fed her through a slot until she passed. Years later, when a new owner moved in, her remains were discovered and the mystery of the servants' deaths was finally pieced together. After repeatedly hearing strange sounds emanating from the

FIGURE 10.1.
Aldridge Mansion

basement, however, the new owner sealed the door shut. Despite the precautions, Gertrude Aldridge's ghost continues to haunt the Aldridge Mansion—ask Erin about her, if you doubt it.

The Stanley Hotel (Estes Park, Colorado): Stephen King was inspired to write *The Shining* after staying at this once-isolated mountain resort in 1973. "The man or woman who insists there are no ghosts [in this world] is only ignoring the whispers of his or her own heart," King wrote in an introduction to the 2001 edition of the classic horror novel. Although he didn't experience any paranormal phenomena during his visit to the Stanley, the room he and his wife stayed in—Room 217—is supposedly haunted by the ghost of a chambermaid who died there in a gas explosion in 1911. The ghosts of the hotel's original owners, F. O. and Flora Stanley, are also said to haunt the premises, alongside a fright of other spooks.

The Borley Rectory (Borley, Essex): This mansion is often called "the most haunted house in England." This is partly due to the paranormal activity reported by residents since the house was built in 1862, and partly due to the efforts of celebrity ghost hunter Harry Price to publicize it as such. Convinced he needed longer than an overnight stay to investigate it, Price rented the house for twelve months. From May 1937 to May 1938, dozens of volunteers observed plenty of strange happenings, including three ghosts that made contact through séances—all of which are documented in Price's book *The Most Haunted House in England.* Although the rectory was destroyed in a fire soon after the conclusion of the year-long stakeout, the site allegedly remains haunted by the spirit of a nun that walks the grounds at night.

112 Ocean Avenue (Amityville, New York): A mother, father, and four of their children were discovered murdered at this nondescript suburban house on Ocean Avenue in Amityville, New York, in 1974. The culprit—the fifth child in the family, Ronald DeFeo, Jr.—was convicted of second-degree murder and is currently serving six concurrent life sentences. A new couple moved into the home the next year, but moved out twenty-eight days later due to a deluge of paranormal activity. Some of the alleged phenomena, such as pig hoofprints in the snow outside their house, are easily explained: A PIG RAN THROUGH YOUR DAMN YARD. Other activity, such as green ectoplasm oozing from a keyhole to the playroom door in the attic, sounds a little freakier. Paranormal investigator Hans Holzer thoroughly investigated the home but did not find any of the elusive ectoplasm. The case remains open.

The Mercado (New York City, New York): This elegant and iconic Midtown hotel (Figure 10.2) has one of the weirdest histories of any building in Manhattan, which is saying something. All sorts of massacres happened at the site even before the building was built. Weird stuff still happens there. Did you know that no other section of New York has more power outages? Now you know! There's also a disproportionate number of traffic accidents on the streets bordering the building, especially on 49th Street. As if all of that wasn't enough, it was also ground zero for the Fourth Cataclysm.

Cashen's Gap (Dalby, Isle of Man): In September 1931, the owner of a farmhouse known as Cashen's Gap heard an animal rummaging in the attic. According to Harry Price's account, James Irving attempted to draw the creature into view by making a series of animal calls—all of which were returned. Even stranger, the unseen creature repeated words! After a few days of this back-and-forth, the creature seemed to achieve fluency. It announced itself as Gef, and told Irving and his wife, "I am a ghost in the form of a weasel and I shall haunt you with weird noises and clanking chains." The spooked couple promptly set out rat poison to rid themselves of the talking creature, with no success. Gef retaliated by killing their turkeys. "I am the eighth wonder of the world," Gef proclaimed from within the wall. He also clarified that he was actually the spirit of a mongoose, not a weasel. They caught sight of Gef a few times, always in passing—Gef was quick, and they usually saw no more than a flash of a bushy tail or its tiny, sharp teeth. Ultimately, Price did not see or even hear the talking mongoose during his investigation, which he chronicled in *The Haunting of Cashen's Gap*. Gef reportedly showed back up after Price left. The mongoose explained to the owners that he'd been on vacation. I'll be straight with you: This was a very weird book. Also, I want a talking pet mongoose. Or a talking weasel. I'm not picky, so long as the damn thing talks.

Patty Tolan is the Ghostbusters' resident municipal historian. Before becoming a metaphysical commando, she worked for the MTA in New York City. She's not sure which job is more dangerous.

CHAPTER 11

Conducting the Metaphysical Examination
A Methodical Examination

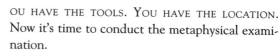

YOU HAVE THE TOOLS. YOU HAVE THE LOCATION. Now it's time to conduct the metaphysical examination.

While your first instinct may be to kick in the doors, ion detectors drawn, you need to slow your roll. We know you're excited to check out the site and put all of that high-tech gear to use, but we must urge caution. This is a highly scientific endeavor. As such, we will use the scientific method, the standardized system of inquiry used by scientists worldwide.

The scientific method begins with a question. For example, you might ask, "Is this house haunted?" Next, you will formulate a hypothesis—in our case, "This house is haunted by a paranormal entity." The hypothesis could be more specific than that, but it doesn't have to be. From there, you will begin to collect data in order to test the veracity of the hypothesis.

Step One: Interview Parapercipient(s)

Gathering data generally starts with an eyewitness interview. If you're investigating a site that's reportedly been haunted for hundreds of years, you may not have access to any of the parapercipients—because they're long since deceased (and possibly ghosts themselves now!). However, we can't stress this enough: Unless you have a firsthand report of the spectral activity, you're probably just wasting your time.

Face-to-face interviews are preferred. However, you can speak to them over the phone if they're located some distance from you. Follow up at a later date in person, prior to setting foot on-site.

Conducting good interviews is a skill anyone can pick up. You don't need to be a journalist, or even a people person—all you need to do is watch a little *Law & Order* or *NYPD Blue*. Interviewing eyewitnesses works best when done in pairs so you can play good ghost hunter, bad ghost hunter. You don't want to get too rough with them, though. Anyone who has seen a ghost—or anyone who even thinks they've seen a ghost—is bound to be in rough shape already.

ALTERNATIVE EXPLANATIONS FOR GHOST SIGHTINGS

According to the SPR, "The unsupported evidence of a single witness does not constitute sufficient ground for accepting an apparition as having a *prima facie* claim to objective reality." That's just a fancy way of saying that witnesses can be mistaken or misleading. During the interview phase of a metaphysical examination, it's important to rule out alternative explanations through careful cross-examination of parapercipients.

Misidentification: Textbooks frequently cite misidentification as the number-one cause of false reports. This may be due to several factors. First and foremost, parapercipients are by and large not trained paranormal investigators. They don't know what to look for. They must rely solely on their senses, which are known to be deceptive. Also, reported paranormal phenomena most frequently occurs in the darkness, whether within a darkened room or at night (or within a darkened room at night). Low-light conditions play tricks on us all the time, as anyone who's gone out with someone they initially met in a dimly lit bar knows.

Hallucinations: You don't need to be feverish or tripping to hallucinate. Many parapercipients report seeing ghosts when going to sleep or waking up. Not coincidentally, this is considered prime time for hallucinating, as the brain drifts through altered states of consciousness on its way to and from the Land of Nod. Hypnagogic hallucinations occur while you're drifting to sleep; hypnopompic hallucinations occur upon waking. Fun fact: Hallucinations *while* you're sleeping are called "dreams."

Naturalistic Explanations: Naturalistic explanations include mice, raccoons, or other animals; household issues such as a settling house, faulty electrical wiring, drafts due to poor insulation, or infrasound from A/C or other sources; and weather such as wind and rain. All of which are SUPER BORING EXPLANATIONS.

Hoax or Fraud: Hoaxes aren't as common an occurrence as skeptics would have you believe. While people may lie about seeing ghosts from time to time, they're certainly not doing it for the attention, which is mostly negative. Admitting you've seen a ghost in front of your peers can be a traumatizing experience. Why anyone would open themselves up to ridicule for no good reason is beyond us! That's why publishing *Ghosts from Our Past: Both Literally and Figuratively: The Study of the Paranormal* is risky. However, it's a risk we have to take . . . FOR SCIENCE.

Source: Hollis Queens. Parapsychology; or, The Science of Psychical Phenomena. *New York City: Harper and Row, 1989.*

Step Two: Evaluate the Evidence

Ready to visit the site? Not so fast. You don't want to go off half-cocked. Always go off full-cocked, as Abby's uncle used to say. We think what he was trying to say is, "You're not prepared for the test unless you've done all the homework."

After conducting your interviews, you may need to restate your hypothesis. Instead of believing the location is haunted, for instance, you could be convinced the parapercipient is hallucinating. It's up to you whether or not you want to continue the metaphysical examination. If you're still reasonably confident you're dealing with potentially paranormal phenomena, the next step involves examining the evidence.

What type of "evidence" are we talking about here? Certainly nothing along the lines of DNA. We wish! It would be great if ghosts left behind hair samples or skin flakes. The closest spirits come to leaving anything behind is ectoplasm, which is incredibly elusive, for reasons we've already discussed.

The typical evidence collected during paranormal investigations is frequently of a far lesser quality than what you may be familiar with on cop shows. Instead of physical evidence, ghost hunters must rely on photographs, audio recordings, and other secondhand sources. Unfortunately, these are all easily faked. Not every spectral photograph or video is fraudulent, but the potential is there. That's enough to invalidate most evidence in the eyes of skeptics.

In the end, any evidence provided by parapercipients should be closely examined and cataloged alongside interview transcripts and the rest of your case files. Don't place too much weight on it, though. The only evidence you can truly trust is that which you collect yourself. If you're still confident you're dealing with a legit spook, then it's time to do your own inspection.

Step Three: Inspect the Location

We advise you to allot as much time as possible for your on-site inspection. You don't need to rent out the location and monitor it for an entire year like Harry Price did with the Borley Rectory, but we do suggest at least one stakeout, which should last eight hours minimum.

Many investigators like to do overnight stakeouts—there's less noise pollution from the outside world, and most people in our line of work have full-time jobs or school during the day. If you're expecting something along the lines of a slumber party, however, you'll be mightily disappointed. Being locked down in a haunted house is *way* more fun than some stupid slumber party. Instead of staying up all night discussing crushes and hitting each other with pillows, you'll be sitting in silence waiting for ghosts!

You should first set up a base camp for your team in one of the rooms (preferably not one where spectral activity has occurred). Establishing a base camp will allow you quick and easy access to all of your equipment, food, and whatever other supplies you've chosen to bring with you. A base camp also provides a common meeting place for everyone on your team, especially in case of emergency or failure of your walkie-talkies.

Ideally, you will have enough investigators on your team for everyone to take a different room in the house. Realistically, finding a single night or day

On Drinking and Ghost Hunting

We're not here to tell you how to live your life. We're not party poopers—we've never even been to a party. However, we must warn you that DRINKING AND GHOST HUNTING DON'T MIX.

That goes the same for any substance capable of impairing your judgment. Not only do you risk injury or death—some of these old haunted houses are dangerous enough as it is—but who's going to believe that you saw a ghost when you smell like you've been rolling down the street with Snoop Doggy Dogg? All you'll have done is make a mockery of parapsychology.

Save the extracurricular activities for later, once you've had a chance to debrief. Personally, we like to kick back after the postmortem with a little hot chocolate with whipped cream on top. Nothing says "success" like a whipped cream mustache! Well, proving that ghosts exist would say "success" even more, but until then, we like to celebrate life's little victories.

when enough people are free to hang out in a haunted house is unlikely to happen. Especially with a large team of ghost hunters, scheduling can be a real pain. Therefore, you'll probably be working with a small crew—again, we recommend a minimum of at least two people for every stakeout.

Draw up a plan of attack based on the number of rooms and the number of investigators, dividing time equally. Every person involved in the investigation should keep their own supernatural stakeout journal. It's also a good idea to rotate in and out of rooms, so as to avoid fatigue and eye strain. Sitting around waiting for something to happen while at full attention is draining. Build in a break schedule. Don't forget to hydrate. And eat! Extreme hunger and dehydration can cause you to hallucinate—and if you hallucinate, you might as well quit and start over again another time.

So what are you waiting around for during a stakeout, exactly? Full-torso apparitions are easy enough to spot. Unfortunately, we're not always so lucky. Or ever so lucky. Therefore, be on the lookout for strange things typically associated with paranormal phenomena.

SIGNS OF POTENTIALLY PARANORMAL PHENOMENA

- Strange lights
- Strange shadows
- Strange noises
- Strange silence

- Strange moving objects
- Strange physical sensations

- Strange smells
- Strange feelings of uneasiness

Basically, it's like the old saying about pornography: You'll know it when you see it. When a ghost brushes up against you, there's no mistaking it. Scientifically confirming what happened, however . . . well, that's a different story.

IMPORTANT!!!!!!!!!!!!!!!!!!!! WHAT TO DO IF YOU SEE A GHOST

First off, DON'T FREAK OUT. This is easier said than done—even after a year of being plagued by the ghost of her next-door neighbor, Erin couldn't sleep without the covers over her face. It might be a foregone conclusion that you're going to freak out, but try not to.

The "rules" governing ghost encounters haven't changed much since Harry Price wrote the first ghost-hunting guide. For reference, here's what Price had to say about what to do when you spot an apparition (updated with modern terminology):

- Do not move, and under no circumstances approach the entity.
- Observe the entity carefully. Take note of its duration and characteristics (e.g., color, form, size, clothing, corporeality) of its appearance.
- If carrying a camera, take photos or video.
- If the entity speaks to you directly, address it respectfully but forcefully. Ascertain as many details of its former or current identity as possible, depending upon its class.
- If the entity makes a threatening gesture or declaration, RUN. Otherwise, do not move until the entity disappears.
- Note the exact method of vanishing. If through an open door, quietly follow while maintaining a safe distance. If through a wall or other solid object, do your best to determine its destination and follow if possible.

Source: Harry Price. The Alleged Haunting of B– Rectory: Instructions for Observers. *London: University of London Council for Psychic Investigation, 1937.*

These are good tips and all, you say, but aren't ghost hunters supposed to do more than just *observe* ghosts? Aren't ghost hunters supposed to . . . shoot them or something?

While some investigators and religious authorities offer exorcisms to rid haunted locations and possessed victims of paranormal entities, such activities fall outside of the purview of the scientifically minded ghost hunter. Besides, we don't currently have paratechnology capable of either dispersing spectral particles or otherwise subduing or dispatching ghosts. While it's possible according to Spectral Field Theory, the development of such tools would require massive amounts of funding—not to mention a technological wizard the likes of which comes along only once in a century, like Thomas Edison.

Step Four: Postmortem

The final step of the metaphysical examination is the postmortem. This is where you will debrief with your crew and write up a report of your findings. Many "weekend" ghost hunters (i.e., amateurs seeking thrills and chills) neglect this step. We don't blame them—who likes doing paperwork? (Put your hand down, Erin.) If you're serious about your investigation, though, you'll put in the time to complete this step. While some teams like to go home and get a good night's rest before writing up a report, we feel that's a mistake. Yes, your brain will be sharper, but you may also forget some of the details.

You can hold your postmortem anywhere. Twenty-four-hour coffee shops are perfect. So are diners like Denny's and Waffle House. It's important for every member of your team to be part of a post-investigation debriefing, which should occur as close to the conclusion of the stakeout or other on-site expedition as possible.

Assign the task of note-taking to whichever team member has the neatest handwriting. Take turns discussing your experiences. No detail is too small—you never know what will become important later. If you took two Tylenol for a headache, that's important. If you felt a draft, even near a cracked window, that's important. If you heard a disembodied voice whisper the name "Utu"—sun god at the temple of Sippar—that's definitely important.

Depending upon what you encountered on-site, you may need to later cross-reference your research with the results of the parapercipient interviews and evidence in order to form a theory about the phenomena you're investigating. If you believe it still might have a paranormal explanation, further research is in order. Start with the classifications found in Chapter 8, and continue with the usual sources listed in our bibliography.

Finally, we've reached the point where you must either verify or reject your hypothesis. Is the location haunted? That's up to you to decide after reviewing the postmortem notes. You may decide you don't have enough evidence to say one way or another, in which case you will need to schedule additional stakeouts, re-interview parapercipients, or submit evidence to specialists for further evaluation.

Concluding Thoughts on Metaphysical Examinations

If your initial forays into paranormal investigation are a bust, don't get frustrated—you're in good company. To paraphrase Nikola Tesla, the scientist does not aim at an immediate result. She does not expect that her advanced ideas will be readily taken up. Her duty is to lay the foundation for those who are to come; her duty is to point the way.

The fact that one hundred years of sustained paranormal research and investigation haven't yielded the same results as, say, the first hundred years of physics is no reason to dump the whole enterprise. "The field which now seems so mysterious will be explored someday, and it will yield—yield very richly," Thomas Edison once said. "I don't know of any man today who is fitted to explore it; but the man will rise when the time is ripe, and he is ripe."

For all we know, the time may be ripe *right now*. And that fabled man (or woman) "fitted to explore" the unknown? It could be us—a couple of nobodies from Battle Creek, Michigan. Or it could be *you*. That's right: YOU COULD BE RIPE.

That totally came out wrong. Sorry. We weren't trying to imply you smelled ripe, dear reader. We're not in the business of pointing fingers (or in this case, using those fingers to plug our noses). If anyone smells ripe, it's probably us. After all, we've been living on Chinese food and Hi-C going on thirteen days now. The other students in the rare book room have taken to avoiding us like the plague, because we probably look like we have the plague. Erin does have a nasty cough . . .

Where were we? Oh, yeah: Just because you don't see a ghost during a metaphysical examination doesn't mean you've wasted your time. If that were the case, we've wasted thousands of hours! Don't let it frustrate you. Desperation has a funny way of driving people to do desperate things. When you're dealing with the paranormal, desperation can turn deadly. Especially if you give up hope on finding evidence of ghosts on this side and instead look for ways to lure them across the barrier.

Most traditional methods of attracting the paranormal, such as Ouija boards, aren't reliable or scientifically proven to work anyway. You may just be setting yourself up for further disappointment. More important, however, you could be placing yourself and others in grave danger. The barrier is in place for a reason. In the next chapter, we'll cover numerous attempts that have been made to coax spectral entities into appearing. As soon as we've taken hobo showers using the ladies'-room sink, that is. See you in a few!

Ectoplasm Cleanup Tips: An Update

While we spent the bulk of this book lamenting the fact that we hadn't gotten our hands on any real ectoplasm to test in a lab, times have changed. Boy, have they ever. Testing requires only a small amount of residue, which can be collected in a four-ounce sample cup from high-density manifestations. The real problem we've run into isn't collecting samples—we now have enough ectoplasm to last a lifetime—it's cleaning the stuff up.

1. In addition to the paratechnology we introduced you to in Chapter 9, every modern-day metaphysical examiner should also have the following equipment at the ready in case of an ecto-contamination incident:
   - Personal protective equipment (e.g., goggles, face masks, disposable rubber gloves)
   - Cleaning solution (i.e., a disinfectant containing bleach, soap, and water)
   - Cleaning supplies (e.g., towels, scrub brushes)
   - Biohazardous waste bags
   - Absorbent material (e.g., sawdust, kitty litter)
   - Four-ounce sterile polypropylene specimen container (available in bulk from online medical supply stores)

2. After donning your personal protective equipment and collecting sample residue, you can begin cleaning up the scene. Sprinkle sawdust (or another absorbent material) onto the ectoplasm. Don't forget to put up a warning sign (Figure 11.1)!

FIGURE 11.1.

3. Wipe up the clumped ectoplasm with disinfectant-soaked towels. Dispose of used towels in labeled biohazard bags and repeat with fresh towels until all liquid ectoplasm has been mopped up.

4. Spray disinfectant onto the area and let set for 15 minutes.

5. Clean the area with unused towels, this time using soap and water. Place towels and all personal protective equipment in biohazard bags.

6. Remove your jumpsuit or other clothing and place in a separate biohazard bag to be laundered. If you're standing around in your undergarments, put on some clean clothes before you get arrested for indecency.

7. Take biohazardous materials to your local waste-collection facility for proper disposal. Not all landfills are currently equipped to handle ecto-contaminated waste, so call ahead.

Adapted from Nell Behrens, "Fast and Easy Spill Cleanup for Bodily Fluids," Good Housekeeping, June 2010, pp. 156-157.

CHAPTER 12

Attracting the Paranormal
Luring Spirits from the Other Side

URPOSEFULLY ATTRACTING THE PARANORMAL—otherwise known as "conjuring"—is a dangerous game. It is also unnecessary. We've seen throughout history that the most malevolent and desperate spirits seem to find their way back through the barrier without anyone's help. As for the rest, they're just chilling on the other side. They're like the bears—and the lions, and the wolves, and every other animal—at the Detroit Zoo. If you catch them at the right time, you might get a good show, but most of the time they're going to be out of sight, napping. Not that ghosts nap, but you know what we mean.

Additionally, you don't know what else is beyond the barrier. What unknown types of Class VI and VII interdimensional entities are just waiting over there for an invitation into our world?

It's like sticking your hand through the bars of a cage, without having any idea what type of animal is on the other side. That's what Thomas Perks, a seventeenth-century schoolteacher, learned when he used an ancient book of black magic to conjure spirits and ended up being terrorized by a fright of Class VI specters.

The most dangerous aspect of conjuring, however, is the damage to the barrier that results from the process. As we've already discussed, weak spots in the barrier already exist in the form of ley lines, which crisscross the

Earth. What we didn't tell you was that ley lines may be even more vulnerable to exploitation by spirits than has been previously believed. (We didn't want to scare you, at least before you were ready.)

The ever-increasing reports of ghosts throughout history are due to more than just the cultural factors and correspondent population growth we examined in Chapter 4. The chances of a full-blown interdimensional crossrip increase with every passing day.

The barrier is losing strength. More and more spirits are returning. Ley lines themselves may, in fact, be due to humanity's meddling with the barrier betwixt life and death. And every time some living numskull breaches the barrier, they risk further weakening the only protection we've got from malevolent entities.

In most cultures throughout history, well-founded cultural taboos against the practice of calling up spirits have kept us from doing further damage to the barrier. Conjuring was illegal for many years in most countries around the world—in England, it was even punishable by death at one time, as decreed by the Witchcraft Act of 1604 and subsequent laws. For most of recorded history, conjuring was relegated to the fringes and attempted by very few.

As you read in the earlier chapter on the history of ghosts, however, mediumship became a fad during the late eighteenth and early nineteenth centuries. Many mediums promised to connect sitters with spirits of their choosing, even if they were still located in the spectral ether—which, of course, required the mediums to breach the barrier and pull unwitting spirits into our world. Luckily for us, the majority of spiritualist mediums were fraudulent. They were swindlers, incapable of doing damage to the barrier. Humanity, it seems, dodged a spectral bullet. Next time a "fad" like spiritualism comes along, we may not be so lucky.

Before We Proceed, a Disclaimer

Attracting the paranormal is not something metaphysical examiners should attempt on their own. The stakes are too high. Experimental probing of the barrier should be undertaken only under the strictest of controlled conditions, conducted by highly trained paratechnicians in a laboratory setting with adequate safeguards in place. You wouldn't let just anyone shoot mon-

Who Calls Up the Dead?

Medium: As we've discussed, this is someone who claims to have the ability to speak directly with spirits (sometimes located on the other side). Also known as a "channel." There is some evidence that certain people may be more sensitive to spectral particles, thus enabling them (under very particular, controlled conditions) to send and receive communications through the barrier. However—and this is an important point glossed over by most spiritualists—*everyone* has the ability to experience paranormal phenomena on this side of the barrier. In other words, you don't need to be a medium to see a ghost.

Shaman: A medium with special "powers" (e.g., healing the sick, divination, etc.). Term used primarily for tribal cultures with strong beliefs in communication with the dead, as well as in New Age circles. Shamans reach out to spirits through trance-like meditations, sometimes induced with hallucinogens such as mushrooms and mescaline. "I start outside and reach the mental through the physical," the modern-day shaman Jim Morrison once said. Can shamans break through to the other side, or are they just tripping? Despite over half a century of laboratory research into consciousness-altering substances, no scientific evidence of its assistance in spirit communication has been uncovered.

Necromancer: In times past, people who called up spirits of the dead through ritual magic were called "necromancers." Nowadays, the term is used almost exclusively in occult circles to describe black magicians who attempt to raise the dead—not the spirits of the dead, but their *actual physical bodies.* In other words, zombies. Speaking to or seeing spirits of the dead is one thing; smelling their decomposing bodies is a whole different ballgame.

keys into space, would you? No. You leave that up to the professionals. The discussions that follow on old-school and new-school conjuring methods are for educational purposes only. In other words: Don't try this at home.

Old-School Methods for Attracting the Paranormal

Frankly, we're dubious about most traditional methods for communicating with ghosts. There's no empirical evidence that any of these methods work—at least not as they're supposed to. It's possible that a ghost or two has dropped by during a Ouija board session, which would be a little like a ten-point buck aimlessly wandering into a deer hunter's backyard. Old-school methods of attracting the paranormal are particularly vulnerable to manipulation by con artists and those seeking to make ghosts "appear" for profit or gain, so it's still important that we review them before moving on to discussion of newer methods.

Rituals and Spells: When Thomas Perks followed the steps in the ancient book of black magic to conjure spirits, he was performing a ritual. Rituals and spells might involve incantations, gestures, or other activities, usually performed within a specific order to achieve a desired result (in this case, the luring of spirits into our world). They may also require special objects. Potions associated with rituals and spells usually require difficult-to-obtain ingredients. While there are documented cases of rituals or spells working—see the Class V case study on the Zugspitze Terror—they are, by and large, ineffectual. There isn't a page in *The Big Book of Blasphemy* that hasn't been read aloud by hundreds of would-be conjurers. Only rarely do such gambits work. Statistically speaking, you're more likely to get hit by lightning. Which is actually much safer than conjuring, to be honest.

Séances: From the French word for "session." As we've stated elsewhere, séances and other such efforts to contact ghosts have been exploited by frauds. It takes more than a dark roomful of six to ten people holding hands to "conjure" a ghost—otherwise, scientists would have long ago called up ghosts in laboratory settings, and you'd be reading their book, not ours.

Ouija Boards: Originally known as "talking boards" and "spirit boards," these cardboard or wooden boards are used to communicate with the dead via a form of assisted automatic writing. Ouija boards come preprinted with the letters of the alphabet, the numbers 0–9, and the words YES, NO, and GOOD-BYE. Sitters, working in a group, collectively rest their fingers lightly on a small, heart-shaped device called a planchette. Spirits guide the users' hands, directing the planchette around the board to spell out messages and answer questions. Many studies have shown that these "spirits" are actually unconscious muscle movements on the part of the sitters, but that hasn't slowed Ouija board sales.

Allegedly based on ancient *Fu Ji* divination boards used in China around 1,100 BC, modern versions of the Ouija board first appeared during the nineteenth-century spiritualist movement. They are now sold in toy stores and novelty shops by Hasbro, which has trademarked the name "Ouija" (if that tells you anything about the authenticity of such boards).

We're not saying they can't be used to communicate with spirits, but what kind of ghost is really going to want to talk to a bunch of fourteen-year-old girls at a slumber party asking questions about their crushes? Actually, that's super creepy to think about.

New-School Methods for Attracting the Paranormal

While traditional methods may occasionally work in spite of themselves, it takes a lot more than a board game from Toys "R" Us or a mass-market paperback of *An Introduction to Ritual Summoning* to reach into the spirit world. It requires the application of science.

Ghost Boxes: Late in Thomas Edison's career, the brilliant inventor began work on a device to contact spirits on the other side. Although he called his would-be invention a "life-unit detector," parapsychologists have come to call such communication devices "ghost boxes."

Scientists and clergy alike warned Edison not to turn his sizable genius on the question of the afterlife, advising him against trespassing "on lands not his own." In a *New York Times* interview in 1921, Edison dismissed the collective concerns about his ghost box, which was still in the blueprint stages.

"I am conducting a laboratory experiment," he said matter-of-factly. He explained that his device would not only be able to detect the disembodied soul—or "life units," in his parlance—but it would pave the way for two-way communication with the dead. He envisioned permanently establishing a line of communication between dimensions.

"If personality exists after what we call death, it is reasonable to conclude that those who leave the Earth would like to communicate with those they have left here," he wrote in *Scientific American.* He vowed not to release more details until he achieved positive results.

Unfortunately, he passed away before unveiling his ghost box. His plans were never found, leaving generations of paranormal investigators to speculate on whether or not Edison ever progressed on the project—and if so, what the results of his testing revealed.

Hundreds of inventors have attempted to make ghost boxes since then. No one has come close to a working model allowing for communication with spirits in the spectral ether. Radio-frequency-based devices are sometimes sold as "ghost boxes," but these knock-off devices are generally limited to picking up transmissions from spirits that have already manifested on this side of the barrier—potentially useful for EVP, but worthless when it comes to reaching the great beyond.

What would it take for a line of communication to be established between our world and the next? And would a working ghost box allow paranormal researchers to lure spectral entities across the barrier for experimentation?

Edison once boasted that there were "half a dozen ways" of approaching the task. Based upon the unfinished nature of his work, however, he must have been missing some key information on the nature of the paranormal that prevented him from developing a working prototype. The missing information, we conjecture, is Spectral Field Theory. Specifically, the covariance of

(a)

covariant

(b) ⟶

UPDATE TO THE REVISED EDITION

Unfortunately, we've been forced to redact large portions of this chapter. We would love—LOVE!—to share all of our research with you, but it's simply not possible. Blacking things out is the best compromise we could come up with to memorialize our work without, you know, watching someone else use it for malicious purposes.

We wish to take this opportunity to express our sincere regret for how our research has been used in the past. We never intended for Spectral Field Theory—and, specifically, our critiques of conjuring—to be used by some deranged bellhop in an attempt to bring about the end of the world. SCREW YOU, ROWAN. SERIOUSLY. SCREW YOU.

While our attorneys don't want us to get any further into that unpleasant business, suffice to say we learned an important lesson the hard way. Which is not as much fun as learning lessons the easy way—through all-night study sessions. There's just something about Chinese food and multiple liters of off-brand pop that softens your brain up so you can cram knowledge in there. Maybe the MSG and caffeine work in combination to break down the soft tissue of the brain, allowing— You know what? Let's let a neurologist work on that one. We're going to stick to what we know best: physics and the paranormal.

If you find a copy of the previous edition of this book, we would advise you to destroy it. Toss it in the recycling bin. Or better yet, fling it into the fireplace, where you can be sure it goes up in smoke. We know, we know: It sounds bad. We're advocating book-burning. Book burning is something we generally, vehemently disapprove of. But in this one, isolated case, it's absolutely necessary.

A Final Word

In conclusion, we hope you've learned a thing or two (or two hundred!) about the paranormal from *Ghosts from Our Past*. We're confident you now have everything you need to conduct your own metaphysical examinations.

Let us take this moment to thank you for reading. We're glad you're still with us. Us ghostheads need to stick together—the path of a metaphysical examiner is not an easy one. Don't ever, for a second, let anyone convince you that parapsychology is a waste of time. It's not a "pseudoscience," as conventionalists would have you believe. It's a science. As anthropologist Margaret Mead once said, "The whole history of scientific advance is full of scientists investigating phenomena that the establishment did not believe were there."

We are on the precipice of new and exciting discoveries as a result of Spectral Field Theory. The scientific inquiry into the paranormal has barely begun. Laboratory experiments with spectral particles will happen sooner rather than later; somewhere, a metaphysical examination will at last uncover conclusive proof of a paranormal entity in the wild. Whether you find ghosts or they find you, we wish you luck. Happy hunting!

New Afterword

Anyone Can Be a Scientist

IN TV AND MOVIES, SCIENTISTS ARE TYPICALLY PORTRAYED AS STOIC FIG-
ures in white lab coats and goggles, heating test tubes with Bunsen burners
for the fun of it. While the stereotype is mostly fiction, Abby has fond memories of dressing up in her mother's white chemistry lab coat and torching
Teenage Mutant Ninja Turtles with lighters.

However, that was only one Michigan preteen's version of science. Yours
may vary!

That's what makes science so great. You don't need a lab coat or goggles;
you don't need any specialized equipment.* You don't even need a degree.
America's First Scientist, Benjamin Franklin, didn't have a scientific degree. Neither did physicist Michael Faraday, naturalist Charles Darwin, or
the Queen of Nineteenth-Century Science, Mary Somerville. If you want
to be a scientist, all you need to do is think like one.

THE GREAT NEWS IS: YOU MAY ALREADY BE DOING THAT.

When Abby was torching those Ninja Turtles, she was—without even
realizing it—following the scientific method. She asked a question: *What
will happen when I put Leonardo's face in the flame of a lighter?* Next, she
formulated a hypothesis: *I believe Leonardo's face will melt.* She gathered
data: *After several seconds in the lighter's flame, Leonardo's face melted into
a goopy green goo, giving off a sweetly pungent odor, verifying the hypothesis.*
After repeating the same steps with Michelangelo, Raphael, and Donatello,
Abby had enough data to postulate a theory: *THE MELTING POINT OF*

---

* *Unless you're going to be splitting atoms. Then you definitely need specialized equipment.*

A NINJA TURTLE IS SOMEWHERE BETWEEN 761 AND 3,591 DE-GREES FAHRENHEIT.

These days, Ninja Turtles aren't so cheap. But that's okay. Even if you don't have any money—even if you can't get a grant, or if your family won't loan you the dough because they already footed the bill for your under-graduate studies and look where that got you—you can still be a scientist.

Some of the greatest scientific minds of all time worked from a place of poverty. Einstein was a clerk in the Swiss Patent Office when he published his theories on the photoelectric effect and special relativity, forever chang-ing the course of physics. In fact, he had only taken the job to stave off unemployment as he pursued his schooling. Einstein was so unremarkable at his day job that he was passed over for promotion, something we can all relate to.

Being terrible at your job doesn't mean you're a bad person. It just means you haven't found the right outlet for your unique skillset. Not to unjustly compare ourselves to Albert Einstein or anything, but we've been passed over for promotion and fired before. Mostly fired. But if your passion truly lies elsewhere, like in SCIENCE, it's almost guaranteed you'll suck at what-ever menial minimum-wage position you're hired for. THAT'S A GOOD THING.

Now that you know that you *can* be a scientist if you want to be, the question becomes: What do you study? Ideally, you'll want to break new ground—to sail uncharted waters, to discover the undiscovered. But is that really possible these days?

Scientists have been getting more and more specialized in their interests, to the point where somebody can devote an entire career to studying a sin-gle giant sequoia. Not to pick on dendrologists again, but that just sounds like a waste of time. Unless the tree is haunted, of course (yes, trees can be possessed). The point remains: Aren't we running out of things to discover?

The short answer is "no."

The long answer is also "no."

There's still plenty of things we don't know, both large and small. We don't know why knuckles crack. We don't know how cats fart without butt cheeks. And we certainly don't have all the answers when it comes to the paranormal.

Now, your particular passion may lie elsewhere . . . but us? We're in this ghost business for the long haul. So what if paranormal investigators continue to be relegated to second-class status in the academic community? Is that going to stop us from being Ghostbusters? Hell, no. Nothing can stop us—not even death. Because we'll do everything in our power to come back to this world and continue our work. Then we'd *really* be breaking new ground.

—*Erin Gilbert, Ph.D., M.S., and Abby L. Yates, Ph.D.*

Epitaph to the Revised Edition

WHEN ABBY ASKED ME TO WRITE THE EPITAPH FOR THE END OF THIS BOOK, I didn't hesitate to answer. Of course I'd do it. I'll do anything for a paycheck, as long as it's not illegal and I don't have to come to the office on Wednesdays. (I'm flexible on the whole "illegal" thing.)

I probably should have hesitated, though.

First, I didn't even know what an epitaph was. Or was it an "epigraph"? Whatever. Not only had I never written one before, but I hadn't even read *Ghosts from Our Past*. They only gave me six months to write the epitaph, which is no time at all when you're training for a hide-and-seek tournament.

If you'd given me one guess as to what their book was about, based upon the title, I'd have said it had to do with regret—the way past decisions, much like spirits of the deceased, can haunt us in the present, creating a toxic web of guilt, anxiety, and remorse, which must be untangled and examined so that we can move forward with our lives, unencumbered by our histories, free from the ghosts of our past.

If I had two guesses, I'd have said the book was probably about actual ghosts. The second option made the most sense, based on all the drawings of ghosts.

Since I didn't have time to read Abby and Erin's book, I decided to see if it had been made into a movie. It hadn't, but I knew there were quite a few movies about ghosts out there. Any one would do.

I asked the girl at the video store which one I should check out. She recommended the one with Patrick Swayze. She also recommended I stream it online, because they "weren't the type of video store that carries movies like that." Needless to say, the selection at the Adult Video Superstore in Chelsea wasn't that "super."

Ten minutes into the Swayze movie, I was already in tears. Patty stopped by my desk. She sat down and started crying too. Then Abby and Erin pulled up chairs, and before long Holtzmann joined us. Everyone was sobbing. At the end, we all went our separate ways and never really spoke about what happened. I kind of wanted to talk about the movie. There were a few things I didn't understand. Was Patrick Swayze's character really a ghost the entire time? And if so, why would a bar hire a ghost as a bouncer?

Of course, I never really needed to watch *Road House* to further my understanding of the paranormal. When you work with the Ghostbusters, you tend to run into ghosts now and again. Occasionally, they even run into you. I have plenty of personal experiences with ghosts to draw on for this epitaph. Unfortunately, I'm saving them for my own ghostbusting memoir, *Kevin Knows Kevin*.

In conclusion, I'll leave you with a few words of wisdom, courtesy of Patrick Swayze: "Be nice . . . until it's time to not be nice." He was talking about bar patrons, but it's also an excellent philosophy for dealing with ghosts. Or clients, who just won't stop calling when there's something weird in their neighborhood. For the last time, Mrs. Ellingson, there's nothing the Ghostbusters can do about the guy on your corner with the cat on his head. Yes, it's strange. But don't call us unless he starts floating, okay? The guy, that is. If the cat's floating, you might want to check with animal control.

Oh, wait. Abby's reading this over my shoulder and says we also handle ghost pets. It's true what they say: You learn something new every day! Especially when you work with smart, talented women. I'm not just typing that because Abby's still reading over my shoulder (although she is). I'm saying it because it's the truth. I could go on longer praising my coworkers, but my index fingers are getting tired. It's almost time to put them to bed for the day.

In closing, if you run into any trouble out there . . . you know who to call. If the trouble is, like, a flat tire, call roadside assistance. For troublesome spirits, call us—the Ghostbusters.

—Kevin, the Ghostbusters' receptionist

Ghostbusting Resources

Now that we've deleted the hundreds of photos of "spectral orbs" that turned out to be dust, we have space to include some additional materials in this edition. From sample interview forms to a comprehensive paranormal dictionary, we're proud to present the resources we wish we'd had at the start of our careers as metaphysical examiners.

Paranormal Quickstart Guide

Paratechnology Tool Kit: The Basics

- Audio Recorder
- Batteries
- Camera
- Carbon Monoxide Detector
- Compass
- EMF Meter
- First Aid Kit
- Flashlight
- Ghost Trap
- Infrasound Monitoring Equipment
- Ion Detector
- Motion Detector
- Night-vision Goggles
- Notebook
- PKE Meter
- Proton Pack
- Toilet Paper
- Walkie-Talkies
- Watch

Conducting a Metaphysical Examination: Step-by-Step

1. Interview Parapercipient(s)
2. Evaluate the Evidence
3. Inspect the Location
4. Postmortem

The Usual Sources: Paranormal Reference Books

Ghosts from Our Past: Both Literally and Figuratively: The Study of the Paranormal by Erin Gilbert and Abby L. Yates

The Great Book of Other Realms by William Ambrose Collins

Encyclopaedia of Psychic Science by Nandor Fodor

The Encyclopedia of Ghosts and Spirits by Rosemary Ellen Guiley

Kemp's Spectral Field Guide by Maureen Kemp

The Heiss Guide to Frightful Entities by Vernon Heiss

Sample Waiver of Liability for Metaphysical Examinations

THIS AGREEMENT COMMENCES ON THIS _____TH DAY OF _____, 20___, between _____ (hereafter referred to as "Client") and _____ (hereafter referred to as "Metaphysical Examiner").

The Client hereby WAIVES ALL CLAIMS OF LIABILITY relating to the activities of the Metaphysical Examiner, their team, or adjuncts, on the premises _____ (address where metaphysical examination is to be conducted) occurring prior to, during, and following the metaphysical examination.

The Client is aware of the risks connected with metaphysical examinations and ASSUMES FULL RESPONSIBILITY for any property damage, losses both financial and emotional, or personal injuries up to, including, and beyond physical death, regardless of whether or not damage, losses, or injury are caused by negligence of the Metaphysical Examiner, their team, or adjuncts.

Examples of damage, losses, and injuries include (but are not limited to): PPSD; property devaluation; loss of life, limb, or sanity; spectral possession; furniture and belongings destroyed due to levitation; ectoplasm stains on carpet and clothing; emotional distress triggered by near-death or out-of-body experiences; or permanent deportation of personal property to other realms.

The Metaphysical Examiner and Client both acknowledge that the metaphysical examination is offered without warranty. So please don't sue if anything goes wrong; the only ones who will get rich are the lawyers.

Printed Name of Client: _____

Client Signature: _____

Printed Name of Metaphysical Examiner: _____

Metaphysical Examiner Signature: _____

Sample form provided for reference only and is not intended for field use. Prior to engaging in work as a metaphysical examiner, seek professional legal assistance from an attorney. Don't worry—they won't dismiss you as a lunatic, as long as you can afford their services.

Is It a Ghost? A Handy Quiz

THINK YOU HAVE WHAT IT TAKES TO BE A GHOSTBUSTER?

Great! Except we're not hiring at the moment. We have, however, prepared a short, ten-question crash course exclusive to the revised edition of *Ghosts from Our Past*.

This quiz is a quick and easy way to test your reading comprehension. It isn't meant to replace the more comprehensive Metaphysical Examination Examination (the MEE, administered through the Kenneth P. Higgins Institute and a handful of other questionably accredited schools of higher learning).

There are no right or wrong answers here—just good and bad answers. If you miss a question or two, don't beat yourself up. We've thrown some trick questions into the mix. Yeah, we tricky.

The only way to know for sure if you're dealing with a ghost is to test for the presence of spectral particles. For this quiz, you won't have a PKE meter. You'll have to rely on your wits. Anyone lacking wits should rely on guts, and if you ain't got any guts then we're a little worried about how your mama raised you.

1. You have moved into a house. For the first week, all was calm. But the second week, the disturbances began—knocking noises inside the walls, mysterious footsteps on the stairs at night, the sounds of a giggling child echoing in the vents. Is it a ghost?

   ANSWER: *Yes. A Class I, from the sound of it. Unless it's just a raccoon with a strange, childlike laugh, which happens more often than you'd expect.*

2. You wake up to find your apartment is in disarray. Pictures have fallen off the walls. A bookshelf has toppled over. Half the dishes are broken and scattered across the kitchen floor. Is it a ghost?

   ANSWER: *No. You either slept through an earthquake, or you're messier than Holtzmann and your apartment is exactly how you left it last night.*

3. A message has materialized in blood on your bedroom wall, threatening you and your family with a plague of locusts unless you pledge your soul to the Lord of the Eternal Harvest. Is it a ghost?

    ANSWER: *Yes. You've been personally targeted by a Class VII entity—quite the honor! You're not a farmer, so the locusts don't pose a threat to any crops, but they could do a number on your potted plants.*

4. While driving on a country road late at night, you pass a horse-drawn carriage that quickly disappears into the fog. Is it a ghost?

    ANSWER: *Depends. Did the horseman holding the reins have a head? If the driver had a head, then it was probably just a regular horse-drawn carriage. If not, then it was definitely a ghost.*

5. Using an old 35mm camera, you take a roll of photographs at your three-year-old niece's birthday party. Upon developing the film, you notice a sinister clown in the background of several of the photos, staring silently into the camera. Is it a ghost?

    ANSWER: *No. That's the clown your sister-in-law hired off Craigslist. Never hire a clown off the Internet. Better yet, never hire a clown.*

6. You hear the howling of a coyote outside your window. Or is it a wolf? You crack the blinds. The yard is empty. But there . . . on the edge of the woods . . . a pair of great, glowing green eyes. Is it a ghost?

    ANSWER: *You'd better believe it! What you've got there is a faery dog, a Class VI entity native to the Scottish Highlands. Sorry—we forgot to tell you that you were in Scotland.*

7. While cruising through the Bering Straight, you spot a ghostly seventeenth-century ship flying a skull-and-crossbones flag, with no visible crew. Your cruise ship's captain attempts to steer around the pirate ship, but it's of no use. As you prepare for a nasty collision, the cruise ship sails right through the spectral ship! Is it a ghost?

ANSWER: *Yes. We kind of gave that one to you, by using the words "ghostly" and "spectral."*

8. Your thirteen-year-old daughter has started speaking in tongues and lighting fires seemingly with her mind. Most disturbingly, she's started sleeping three feet above her bed. Is it a ghost?

   ANSWER: *Possibly—if she's possessed, that is. Alternatively, she may be exhibiting telekinetic powers, which commonly manifest in young adults her age, according to some paranormal experts. Either way, keep a fire extinguisher handy.*

9. Every time you descend the steps into the basement of your Victorian home, you get the chills. You felt a hand on your shoulder and heard your name whispered down there last week, although nobody was there when you turned around. Is it a ghost?

   ANSWER: *Yes. While further investigation is necessary, this has all the makings of a Class III haunting.*

10. For the past several months, your morning toast has come out either barely warm, or else burnt to a crisp as if in hell's oven—all on the same toaster setting. Is it a ghost?

    ANSWER: *Even if it is, the issue can be solved by simply buying a new toaster.*

Kemp's Spectral Classification Table

Class	Form	Sentience	Intelligence	Malevolence
I	Indefinite	No	Low	Low
II	Human (Partial)	Yes	Low to Moderate	Low
III	Human—former identity not established	Yes	Moderate	Moderate to High
IV	Human—former identity established	Yes	Moderate	Moderate to High
V	Non-human	Yes	Low	High
VI	Non-human	Yes	Low	Very High
VII	Varies	Yes	High	Extreme

Partial ectoplasmic manifestations such as vapors and mists, as well as other sensory stimuli (disembodied voices, enigmatic knocking sounds, spectral orbs, etc.)

Spectral hands, animated lips, and other substantial physical compositions created out of ectoplasm by spirits; also includes definite physical interactions with this world, such as levitating objects

Significantly more developed than Class II entities, though may be missing body parts (legs, arms, head, etc.); also includes possessions

Identical to Class III entities, except the spirit's mortal progenitor has been positively established

Thought to be composites of residual PKE, these entities have no recognizable connection to their former lives in physical shape, thought, or behavior

Ectoplasmic manifestations from the spirits of non-human terrestrial, extraterrestrial, and lesser interdimensional life forms; most commonly animals or animalistic entities

Metaspecters; very powerful interdimensional entities with god-like powers capable of assuming multiple forms through the manipulation of ectoplasm

Source: Maureen Kemp. Kemp's Spectral Field Guide. *New York: Doubleday, 1984.*

Parapercipient Interview Form

Parapercipient Name: _____

Date of Birth: _____

Legal Guardian (if under 18): _____

Phone Number: _____

Date and Time of Alleged Paranormal Activity: _____

Location of Alleged Paranormal Activity (circle one):

Single-Family House • Multi-Family House • Apartment • Theater • Inn/Hotel

• Prison/Jail • Graveyard • Hospital • Battlefield • Restaurant • Office Build-

ing • Hair or Nail Salon • Other: _____

Address: _____

Date Built (if known or applicable): _____

List a brief history of paranormal phenomena at the location, excluding the most

recent occurrence: _____

_____

_____

_____

Have any tragic deaths or traumatic events occurred at the location? _____

_____

_____

_____

_____

Describe the paranormal phenomenon you personally experienced, in as much

detail as possible: _____

_____

_____

_____

_____

_____

_____

_____

Did anyone else witness the activity? If so, list contact information: _____

_____

_____

_____

Were you under the influence of drugs, stimulants, or alcohol at the time of the para-

normal phenomenon? Include any prescription and over-the-counter medications:

_____

_____

Have you or any member of your family ever been diagnosed or judged legally

mentally incompetent? _____

_____

_____

_____

Have you experienced paranormal or unexplained phenomena in the past?

_____

_____

_____

_____

* * * * * * * * FOR METAPHYSICAL EXAMINER USE ONLY * * * * * * * *

Metaphysical Examiner Name: _____

Date of Interview: _____

Parapercipient Body Language (e.g., shifty eyes, crossed arms, excessive sweating,

etc.): _____

_____

_____

Additional Notes: _____

_____

_____

_____

_____

_____

_____

_____

_____

_____

Supernatural Stakeout Journal

Name: _____ Date of Stakeout: _____

Other Metaphysical Examiners On-Site (each examiner should keep their own

journal): _____

Address: _____

Map of Location:

Room #1 (note size, distinguishing features):

_____

_____

_____

Room #2 (note size, distinguishing features):

_____

_____

_____

Room #3 (note size, distinguishing features):

_____

_____

_____

Etc.

**** FOR EACH PARANORMAL INCIDENT, ****
**** FILL OUT THE FOLLOWING SECTION ****

Start Time: _____   End Time: _____

Type of Phenomenon (circle all that apply):

Visual • Auditory • Tactile • Olfactory • Gustatory • Psychical

Equipment Readings (multiple measurements recommended):

Carbon Monoxide Level: _____ PPM   (Time: _____)

Electromagnetic Field: _____ Hz   (Time: _____)

Infrasound Level: _____ Hz   (Time: _____)

Ions: + / – / None   (Time: _____)

Psychokinetic Energy: Yes / No   (Time: _____)

Other: _____

_____

Full Description: _____

_____

_____

_____

_____

_____

_____

_____

Non-Paranormal Explanations for Phenomenon (circle all that apply):

House Settling • Mice, Raccoons, or Other Animals • Faulty Electrical

Wiring • Plumbing • Infrasound from A/C or Other Source • Poor Insulation

• Weather Event • Hallucination • Fraud • Hoax • Misidentification •

Exaggeration • Tricks of the Eye • Other: _____

Explanation: _____

_____

_____

**** IF A HAUNTING IS SUSPECTED, FILL OUT THE BELOW FORM ****

Agent Properties:

Humanoid • Non-humanoid • Unknown or N/A
Anchored • Free-roaming • Unknown or N/A
Full-torso • Partial-torso • No Torso • Unknown or N/A
Ethereal • Corporeal • Unknown or N/A
Grounded • Floating • Free-floating • Unknown or N/A
Individual • Composite • Unknown or N/A
Possessing • Animating • Inhabiting • N/A

Other: _____

_____

_____

Physical interactivity:

T1 • T2 • T3 • T4 • T5

Circle the entity class or classes that may apply:

I • II • III • IV • V • VI • VII

The Devil's Dictionary

Paraterminology You Need to Know

Agent: We don't mean an FBI agent, like Fox Mulder. Parapsychologists use the term "agent" to refer to the primary actor in a metaphysical examination (usually an entity). For cases involving poltergeists, the agent is the human around which the poltergeist activity is centered.

Amulet: Gems, scarabs, or other paratrinkets thought to ward off malevolent specters. Such spectral bling is of dubious practical value.

Apport: A solid object teleported from another location, usually from the spectral ether. Conversely, a deport is an object teleported away from a location. Not to be confused with ectoplasmic manifestations.

Astral Body: Some paranormal experts believe in the astral body, a sort of middle ground between the physical body and the soul. Believers in astral bodies point to out-of-body experiences as proof. During an astral projection, the astral body is said to leave the physical body and take flight, often soaring around the globe or traversing the galaxy in an invisible state. We read one account where an astral-projection proponent believed she had visited Saturn and returned to her body on Earth in under sixty minutes! Such a journey would have required her to travel over twice the speed of light—an impossibility, according to most physicists. Even if astral bodies exist, it's unlikely we can just take them out for joyrides to the stars and back.

Astral Projection: See *Astral Body*.

Automatic Writing: Spirit-directed writing; a form of para-transferral embodiment. Ectoplasm allows spirits to physically manipulate possessed parapercipients' bodies.

Barrier: The durable but not impenetrable wall separating our world from the spectral ether.

Channel: See *Medium*.

Clairvoyance: A type of extrasensory perception. From the French words *clair* ("clear") and *voyance* ("vision"). Clairvoyants are said to be able to psychically view both the past and the future, as well as remotely view objects and events in the present that would otherwise be inaccessible. Believers in clairvoyance are unable to adequately explain just how such powers work, in a scientific context. It appears clairvoyance is also French for "b.s."

Control: A spirit that acts as a guide to the spectral ether. Common during the heyday of the spiritualist movement, but uncommon in today's DIY world. Most paranormal investigators and mediums prefer to cut out the middleman when possible.

Deport: See *Apport*.

Direct Voice Phenomena (DVP): Spirits speaking without the aid of a medium.

Direct Writing: Unlike automatic writing, direct writing occurs when a spirit takes control of a writing device with the aid of ectoplasm, rather than possessing someone and using their hand. Which is probably for the best—using someone else's hand is just creepy.

Divination: The art of prophecy. Fortune-tellers make predictions based on divine inspiration, which is occasionally said to come from spectral entities. Divination takes many forms, among them a branch centered around the use of flour. In ancient Greece, occult Paula Deens baked slips of paper with aphorisms (often predictive in nature) into breads, cookies, and cakes. Baking them somehow "sealed" the fortunes. As you might have guessed by now, fortune cookies are actually a modern-day form of this ancient practice (known as "aleuromancy"). Every time you crack one open, you're practicing divination! Another fun fact: Fortune cookies are served in Chinese restaurants in the U.S. and around the world—everywhere, that is, except China. Which makes us feel like we're participating in some sort of cultural-appropriation sham (though that's not going to stop us from eating them). But back to divination: Does it work? As the Magic 8 Ball says, "My sources say no."

Drop-in Communicator: Séances are usually conducted with the intent of reaching a particular spirit. When a different ghost makes an appearance, the unwanted visitor is said to be a drop-in communicator. Such uninvited guests may offer their skills to mediums as controls. Then again, they might just spit ectoplasm in your face and give you a spectral wedgie. Drop-in communicators should not be trusted. If you ordered a pizza from Papa John's, and a delivery person in an unmarked van arrived with a pizza from an anonymous pizza joint, would you eat it? Depends on how hungry you are.

Ectoplasm: Spectral foam generated through significant coupling of spectral and Standard Model particles. Negatively charged ectoplasm allows psychokinetic energy–based entities to interact physically with our world. Residue is generally green or white in appearance.

Electronic Voice Phenomena (EVP): Recorded voices, thought to be transmissions from ghosts or other entities. Usually recorded on magnetic tape and heard only on playback.

Entity: Interdimensional manifestations originating from the spectral ether.

Exorcism: When an entity takes control of a human being, an object, or a site such as a house, a request is often made for it to be expelled via an exorcism. Unless you don't mind that your roommate Brittany is possessed. Maybe the ghost actually empties the dishwasher once in a while. Exorcisms may work from time to time, but scientifically grounded means of entity disposal are the only techniques used by professional paranormal exterminators.

Extrasensory Perception (ESP): So-called powers of the mind that seemingly transcend the senses. See *Clairvoyance* and *Telekinesis*.

Fortune-Telling: See *Divination*.

Fright: Collective noun for a group of spectral entities (i.e., "a fright of ghosts").

Ghost: Traditionally, spirit energy of a deceased life form that has returned to this universe from the spectral ether. Composed of psychokinetic energy and, in physical form, ectoplasm. The word "ghost" is also used to describe any type of paranormal entity, including interdimensional entities— You know what? Do we really need to define this for anyone?! WHAT DO YOU THINK WE'VE BEEN DOING FOR THE PAST COUPLE OF HUNDRED PAGES?!!

Ghost Hunt: See *Metaphysical Examination.*

Ghost Vehicles: Spectral ships, airplanes, and other vehicles are rare but notable. One of the most famous is the *Flying Dutchman*, a seventeenth-century ship that glows deep red with a crew of ghostly pirates. In some instances, ghost vehicles are thought to be composed entirely of ectoplasm, being the handiwork of one or more returned human spirits—after all, Ford Tempos don't have spirits. In other instances, vehicles may be possessed by interdimensional entities.

Ghostly Images on TV (GIOTV): Spectral images seen or heard on the television. And, no, *The X-Files* doesn't count.

Goat: Term used in academic circles for nonbelievers in the paranormal. See also *Sheep.*

Guide: See *Control.*

Haunted: A location with recurrent paranormal phenomena is said to be "haunted." People, animals, and inanimate objects possessed or inhabited by spirits are also sometimes referred to as being haunted.

Interdimensional: From outside our universe. By their very nature, paranormal entities are considered interdimensional since they originate in a higher dimension (see *Spectral Ether*). Some academics use the term "transdimensional."

Levitation: The ability to float in the air in apparent defiance of the laws of physics. Most ghosts can levitate at will. While some paranormal experts believe people and objects can levitate as well, we're less convinced such a thing is possible without the aid of PKE and/or ectoplasm. That's not to say it won't ever be possible: Less than a hundred years ago, the idea that the human race would land on the moon was considered impossible. Some say it still hasn't happened.

Materialization: The act of creating physical matter seemingly out of nothing. In paranormal terms, an entity is said to materialize in space-time when it takes shape using ectoplasm, which is generated through a reaction between our universe and the spirit's PKE.

Medium: Any person who claims to have a direct conduit to spirits or the spectral ether.

Metaphysical: See *Paranormal.*

Metaphysical Examination: A paranormal investigation or "ghost hunt." Usually focused on a single location, and conducted by a team of trained metaphysical examiners with the express purpose of confirming or denying a paranormal presence.

Mortal Progenitor: A spirit's former identity as a living being.

Near-Death Experience (NDE): An out-of-body experience reported by persons who have come close to death. You might even say they've come NEAR DEATH. Experients report a sense of floating out of their body, as well as a host of other phenomena such as dark tunnels, bright lights, the spirits of deceased relatives, and the presence of a supreme being welcoming them to the spirit world (i.e., the spectral ether). Of patients whose hearts have stopped but were revived, 8 to 12 percent report experiencing one or more classic NDE components. Previously, NDEs were about the only way to glimpse the other side. We got our own peek at it, however, when we went through a portal (detailed in *A Glimpse into the Unknown*, a sample of which appears at the end of this book)!

Other Side: See *Spectral Ether.*

Ouija Board: Cardboard or wooden board used for communication with the dead. A popular party game for children and teenagers. At least that's what we hear.

Out-of-Body Experience: See *Astral Projection* and *Near-Death Experience.*

Paranormal: Beyond ordinary sensory perceptions or established scientific laws. Some paranormal experts make a distinction between the paranormal, the supernatural, and the metaphysical; we think they're full of it. Not only are these terms interchangeable, but they're also just placeholders. On a long enough timeline, every element of the paranormal will either be incorporated into the scientific canon or discarded.

Paranormal Investigation: See *Metaphysical Examination.*

Parapercipient: One who experiences paranormal activity firsthand.

Parapsychology: The study of paranormal phenomena. The three main fields of study are spirits of the dead, clairvoyance, and telekinesis. Unlike other branches of scientific inquiry, parapsychology has existed mostly outside the walls of academia. Duke University is one of the few institutes for higher learning to have housed a parapsychology department (the now defunct Parapsychology Laboratory). Since experiments require funding—difficult to obtain without university backing—parapsychologists must often rely on theories rather than experimental studies and trials.

Paratainment: Derogatory word for ghost tours, TV ghost-hunting shows, and other paranormal-related entertainment. Don't use it around serious paranormal investigators, unless you want to get jumped in the parking lot later. Just kidding—paranormal investigators aren't that dangerous. It's the ghosts you have to worry about.

Paratechnology: Any technology used with the intent of observing or affecting paranormal activity.

Para-transferral Embodiment: Possession of a living being or object by an interdimensional entity. Ectoplasm appears to be a necessary component of possession, although it's entirely possible that spirits may be able to manipulate living and inanimate hosts solely using psychokinetic energy. An unknown number of possessed persons are unfortunately misdiagnosed with mental illnesses such as epilepsy, schizophrenia, or mania. Many everyday objects, from televisions to hair dryers, are also capable of being possessed. When taking control of an object, an entity is said to be animating it; when permanently bonded to an object, an entity is said to be inhabiting it.

Phone Calls from the Dead (PCFTD): Spectral voices heard over the telephone. Before you ask: TFTD (Texts from the Dead) is not a real thing. Neither is FFTD (Facebook from the Dead) or SFTD (Snapchat from the Dead). Smartphones and computer technology are frustratingly immune to spectral interference.

Planchette: See *Ouija Board*.

Plane: Another word for "universe," this term is generally used in a nonscientific context. Instead of "planes," physicists speak of higher dimensions and other universes beyond ours.

Poltergeist: "Poltergeist" is a German word meaning "angry spirit." In the past, the word has been used to describe any destructive entity whose behavior includes: noises; fires; tossing-around or levitation of objects; bites, scratches, or pinches; and other antagonistic behavior. In the twentieth century, the term came to be associated with a very particular type of haunting, centered around a living agent (almost always a young girl at the onset of puberty). According to the poltergeist hypothesis, paranormal phenomena in such cases aren't caused by spectral entities. Rather, they are a manifestation of the agent's own telekinetic powers. Of course, most poltergeist behaviors—loud noises, thrown objects, crap being set on fire—are also associated with regular teenagers. Is an extra floating lamp or two that much worse?

Possession: See *Para-transferral Embodiment*.

Postcognition: See *Retrocognition*.

Precognition: Extrasensory awareness of future events. Opposite of retrocognition. See also *Clairvoyance*. Or, if you possess precogitive abilities, envision yourself having already read that entry.

Psychic or Psychical: In the nineteenth and twentieth centuries, these terms were synonymous with "paranormal." Sometimes abbreviated as "psi" or the Greek letter Ψ. Today, the word "psychic" refers to persons with telekinetic abilities.

Psychokinesis: See *Telekinesis*.

Psychokinetic Energy (PKE): Spectral particles with no measurable material substance (i.e., "spirit energy").

Radio Voice Phenomena (RVP): Spectral voices heard over the radio.

Reincarnation: The idea that the human spirit or soul can be "reborn" into a physical body. Reincarnation may either be in the form of a person, animal, or other living creature, depending upon the school of thought. Proof is often offered in the form of past-life regression therapy, during which patients "remember" buried thoughts from past lives. Though belief in reincarnation is central to some religions, such as Hinduism, there is no conclusive evidence that reincarnation is possible. Purported cases may involve spirits of the dead possessing the living via para-transferral embodiment.

Remnant: The typical remnant is described as "repeating" (i.e., continuously re-living the final moments of its earthly life, like a song on repeat for eternity). Remnants are thought to be human spirits that have not crossed over into the spirit realm. While we once thought it was scientifically impossible for spirits to physically manifest on this side of the barrier without first crossing over, recent evidence has us rethinking remnants and their relationship to Spectral Field Theory.

Remote Viewing: See *Clairvoyance.*

Retrocognition: Extrasensory awareness of past events (also known as "postcognition"). Opposite of precognition. Frankly, quite a bit less impressive than seeing into the future. We suppose it would be a cool ability for a detective? See also *Clairvoyance.*

Scientific Method: A standardized system of inquiry utilized by modern-day scientists around the world. The basic steps of the scientific method are: Ask a question; formulate a hypothesis; gather data from observations or experiments; evaluate the data; and verify or reject the hypothesis.

Séance: Gathering of persons for the express intent of contacting spirits of the dead. Led by a medium, and typically attended by a circle of four to twelve sitters (or witnesses) who link hands around a table.

Sheep: Term used in academic circles for believers in the paranormal. See also *Goat.*

Sitters: See *Séance.*

Spectral Ether: A dimension beyond space-time, populated by spectral particles (i.e., psychokinetic energy). Also called the "other side." See also *Spectral Field Theory.*

Spectral Field Theory: Gauge field theory proposed by Drs. Erin Gilbert and Abby L. Yates, which unites the metaphysical world with the physical world using theoretical physics to explain spectral particles and their behavior. See also *Spectral Ether, Psychokinetic Energy, Ectoplasm.*

Spectral Foam: See *Ectoplasm.*

Spirit Cabinet: No, a "spirit cabinet" isn't a cupboard where you keep your booze. A spirit cabinet is a hollow wooden cabinet sometimes used during a séance to "give spirits privacy." In practice, a medium is locked in the cabinet or curtained off inside it, giving them free rein to conjure ectoplasmic manifestations unimpeded by observers. Spirit cabinets also give fraudulent mediums room to produce melons from nowhere.

Spirit Photograph: Photos purporting to show manifestations of spirits, occasionally when such ghosts are not visible to the naked eye. One of the most famous spirit photographs, taken by Boston jeweler William Mumler, supposedly captured the spirit of Abraham Lincoln, hands poised upon his unsuspecting widow Mary Todd's shoulders. Mumler's handiwork is laughably fraudulent to the modern eye, although it created quite a stir in the nineteenth century. Today, we know that even the most corporeal of entities is difficult to photograph. Full-torso humanoids may show up as glowing orbs; other spectral entities may not show up at all.

Spiritualism: A nineteenth-century movement based on the belief that the spirit survives bodily death. Jump-started by the Fox sisters and sustained by hundreds of mediums throughout the U.S. and Europe well into the 1900s. Although a small number of spiritualists remain as part of an organized religion, the public's fascination with spiritualism ended shortly after World War I amidst accusations of fraud.

Spirit World: See *Spectral Ether.*

Supernatural: See *Paranormal.*

Survival Hypothesis: The idea that human consciousness survives bodily death in some form.

Table Tipping: A specialized type of séance held around a wooden table. Instead of linking hands, sitters rest their hands on the table and wait for a spirit to move (or "tip") the table.

Talisman: See *Amulet.*

Telekinesis: A psychic ability allegedly permitting manipulation of physical objects with the mind. Telekinetic psychics are famous for bending spoons, lifting tables and chairs, and other (mostly underwhelming) psychic phenomena. Bending a spoon isn't that impressive—Abby can do that one-handed. ABBY, STOP BENDING ALL OF OUR SPOONS. Telekinesis is considered one of the three primary branches of parapsychology, although it falls outside the scope of this book except in regard to alleged poltergeist behavior. Telekinesis is also known as "psychokinesis," although we prefer to use the former term to distinguish it from psychokinetic energy.

Teleportation: Instantaneous paranormal transportation of objects or persons from one location to another. Popular with mediums in the late nineteenth century (see *Apport*). Quantum teleportation of information between previously entangled particles is possible. However, even the most open-minded theoretical physicists consider teleportation of larger physical objects to be an impossibility. In fact, some party pooper in the field of quantum physics even coined a "no-teleportation theory" (seriously, that's what they called it). Looks like we won't be getting *Star Trek* transporters anytime soon.

Theory: Scientific theories are well-tested or heavily backed explanations for phenomena. If a better theory emerges, it replaces the older theory over time. The Earth was once thought to be flat; when better information became available, scientists changed their collective mind. No theory is so well established that it can't be replaced as necessary. You hear that, Einstein? Your special theory of relativity ain't *that* special.

Time Travel: Some astral projection proponents believe the astral body can travel forward and backward in time—that is, without regard to the fourth dimension. Good luck with that!

Xenoglossy: When someone speaks or writes in a language unknown to them, they are said to be practicing "xenoglossy." In a paranormal context, this involves either para-transferral embodiment or automatic writing. While xenoglossy is undoubtedly a real phenomenon, it's difficult to verify that any particular parapercipient has zero familiarity with a foreign language. Fraudulent mediums may not be forthcoming about the four years of Spanish they took in high school; other xenoglossy practitioners may have picked up another language when they were children and forgotten it. While the latter sounds farfetched, many skeptics would say para-transferral embodiment is far-fetched. We wouldn't say that, of course.

NOTES

We've provided some space for you to take notes. Please don't use it to make plans for destroying the world. Four cataclysms are plenty!

_____

_____

_____

_____

_____

_____

_____

_____

_____

_____

_____

_____

_____

_____

_____

_____

_____

_____

NOTES

NOTES

NOTES

NOTES

NOTES

NOTES

NOTES

Bibliography

Agrippa, Heinrich Cornelius. Trans. by James Freake. Edited and annotated by Donald Tyson. *Three Books of Occult Philosophy.* Woodbury, MN: Llewellyn Publications, 1993.

Anderson, Jean. *The Haunting of America.* Boston, MA: Houghton Mifflin Company, 1973.

Auerbach, Loyd. *ESP, Hauntings, and Poltergeists.* Boston, MA: Warner Books, 1986.

Bandette, Josephine. *The Occult Encyclopaedia: In Thirteen Volumes.* Cambridge, MA: Harvard University Press, 1919.

Barbanell, Maurice. *Across the Gulf.* London: Psychic Press, 1945.

Barnard, Guy Christian. *The Supernormal: A Critical Introduction to Psychic Science.* London: Rider & Co., 1933.

Big Book of Blasphemy, The. N.p.: n.p., n.d.

Broome, Doris. *Fairy Tales from the Isle of Man.* London: Penguin Books, 1951.

Celtic Magazine, The. "Tales of the Water-Kelpie." XIL (1887).

Chance, P. "Parapsychology Is an Idea Whose Time Has Come." *Psychology Today* 7, October 1973.

Collins, William Ambrose. *The Great Book of Other Realms.* New York: Ballantine, 1991.

Dutton, Archibald. *Systema Unnaturae.* London: J. W. Bouton, 1787.

Elis, Marcus. "Ley Lines and Elis Vortex Theory." *Scientific American* 232:6 (1980).

Finucane, R. C. *Ghosts: Appearances of the Dead & Cultural Transformation.* Amherst, NY: Prometheus Books, 1996.

Fisk, Eleanor. *Fiends with Benefits: True Stories of Paranormal Love*. Garden City, NY: Doubleday, 1981.

Fodor, Nandor. *Encyclopaedia of Psychic Science*. Secaucus, NJ: Citadel Press, 1966.

Glanvill, Joseph. *Saducismus Triumphatus: or, Full and Plain Evidence Concerning Witches and Apparitions*. London: James Collins, 1681.

Goodstein, David. *States of Matter*. Mineola, NY: Dover Publications, 1985.

Gottfried, Kurt, and Victor Weisskopf. *Concepts of Particle Physics Vol. I*. London: Oxford University Press, 1984.

Green, Andrew. *Ghost Hunting: A Practical Guide*. London: Garnstone Press, 1973.

Guiley, Rosemary Ellen. *The Encyclopedia of Ghosts and Spirits*. New York: Facts on File, 1992.

——————. *Harper's Encyclopedia of Mystical & Paranormal Experience*. San Francisco: Harper San Francisco, 1991.

Haining, Peter. *A Dictionary of Ghosts*. New York: Dorset Press, 1993.

Handbook for the Recently Deceased. The Neitherworld: Handbook for the Recently Deceased Press, n.d.

Heiss, Vernon. *The Heiss Guide to Frightful Entities*. New York: Macmillan Publishers, 1928.

——————. *The Heiss Guide to Frightful Funguses*. New York: Macmillan Publishers, 1931.

Hogg, James. *The Three Perils of Man; or, War, Women, and Witchcraft*. London: Longman, Hurst, Rees, Orme, and Brown, Paternoster-Row, 1822.

Hole, Christina. *Haunted England: A Survey of English Ghost-lore*. New York: C. Scribner's Sons, 1941.

Holzer, Hans. *Murder in Amityville*. New York: Belmont Tower Books, 1979.

Inman, Alexandre. *It's Your Afterlife: A Handbook for Lost Souls*. Nashville, TN: Thomas Nelson, Inc., 1989.

Irwin, Harvey J. *An Introduction to Parapsychology*. 2nd ed. Jefferson, NC: McFarland and Company, 1994.

Kemp, Maureen. *Kemp's Spectral Field Guide*. New York: Doubleday, 1984.

—————. *Never Lonely: A Life Amongst the Spirits.* New York: Doubleday, 1993.

Kurtz, Paul. *A Skeptic's Handbook of Parapsychology.* Buffalo, NY: Prometheus Books, 1985.

Landau, L. D., and E. M. Liftschitz. *The Classical Theory of Fields.* 2nd ed. Oxford: Pergamon Press, 1971.

LeBlanc, Kati. *The Oxford Companion to the Necronomicon.* Oxford, UK: Oxford University Press, 1991.

Leroux, R. L. *Corporeal Apparitions of the Northeastern United States.* Boston: Little, Brown and Company, 1973.

Lowrey, Wendy. "Mass Turbulence Events in the Tri-State Region, 1940–1950." *Journal of Unexplained Things, Explained,* 20:3 (1987).

Marshall, Edward. " 'No Immortality of the Soul' says Thomas A. Edison." *New York Times.* October 2, 1910.

McGrayne, Sharon Bertsch. *Nobel Prize Women in Science: Their Lives, Struggles, and Momentous Discoveries.* Secaucus, NJ: Carol Pub. Group, 1993.

Meritt, Christopher. "ESP and Trepanation: A Curious Case Study." *American Parapsychologist* 74:1(1992).

New York Times. "Soul Has Weight, Physician Thinks." March 11, 1907.

Nickell, Joe, and Robert A. Baker. *Missing Pieces: How to Investigate Ghosts, UFOs, Psychics and Other Mysteries.* Buffalo, NY: Prometheus Books, 1992.

Patrick, Jeremy. "Kemp's Spectral Field Guide: Ten Years Later." *Newsweek,* July 7, 1995.

Peebles, Jim. *Principles of Physical Cosmology.* Princeton, NJ: Princeton University Press, 1993.

Pliny the Younger. *Letters.* Trans. by William Melmoth. Rev. by W. M. L. Hutchinson. London: William Heinemann, 1931.

Price, Harry. *The Alleged Haunting of B— Rectory: Instructions for Observers.* London: University of London Council for Psychic Investigation, 1937.

—————. *Confessions of a Ghost-Hunter.* London: Putnam & Co., 1936.

—————. *The End of Borley Rectory.* London: Harrap & Co. Ltd., 1946.

—————. *The Most Haunted House in England: Ten Years' Investigation of Borley Rectory*. London: Longmans, Green & Co. Ltd., 1940.

Price, Harry, and R. S. Lambert. *The Haunting of Cashen's Gap*. London: Methuen & Co. Ltd., 1936.

Queens, Hollis. *Parapsychology; or, The Science of Psychical Phenomena*. New York: Harper and Row, 1989.

Reznor, Curtis. *I Came Back Haunted: Near-Death Experiences*. Cleveland, OH: Halo Books, 1961.

Ryder, Lewis H. *Quantum Field Theory*. 2nd ed. Cambridge, UK: Cambridge University Press, 1996.

Shankar, R. *Principles of Quantum Mechanics*. 2nd ed. New York: Kluwer Academic/Plenum Publishers, 1994.

Sidgwick, A., and E. M. Sidgwick. *Henry Sidgwick: A Memoir*. London: Macmillan, 1906.

Stenger, Victor J. *Physics and Psychics: The Search for a World Beyond the Senses*. Buffalo, NY: Prometheus Books, 1990.

St. Pierre, Alexander. *An Introduction to Ritual Summoning*. London: Mifflin & Sons, 1906.

U.S. News & World Report. "A Stepchild of Science Starts to Win Friends." July 31, 1978.

Walker, Thomas. "The Beheading (and Reheading) of Herculanus of Preguai." *Journal of Medieval Martyrdom* 3:12 (1982).

Wangsness, Roald K. *Electromagnetic Fields*. 2nd ed. New York: John Wiley & Sons, 1986.

Wilson, Ian. *In Search of Ghosts*. London: Headline Book Publishing Ltd., 1995.

Acknowledgments

In the first edition, we thanked the University of Michigan's library staff, Chen at Tomorrow's Teriyaki, and Professor Alderman. We realize, now, that we left a lot of people out, including our families—an inadvertent and regrettable error, of course.

Our editor, Andrew, would like to thank Paul Feig, Katie Dippold, and Cira Sims; Virginia King and the entire crew at Sony Pictures; Ivan Reitman, Eric Reich, and the rest of the Ghostheads at Ghost Corps; Amy Pascal and Pascal Pictures; Matt Inman and all his minions at Crown Publishing and Random House Audio; James Maxwell; Brandi Bowles at Foundry Literary + Media; and Kristen Wiig, Melissa McCarthy, Kate McKinnon, Leslie Jones, Bill Murray, and Chris Hemsworth for their inspiring performances. Special thanks to Dan Aykroyd and Harold Ramis for laying such a brilliant foundation. Andrew should also probably thank Erin and Abby for graciously making room on the cover for him even though they did, like, 97 percent of the work.

Erin would like to thank Abby.

Abby would like to thank Erin.

Shoot! We're out of space and, once again, we totally forgot to thank our families for their love and support. And we forgot to thank the rest of the Ghostbusters, without whom we wouldn't have nearly half as much fun as we do saving the world. Oh, well. We'll make space in the next book for everyone! Promise.

Photography Credits

page 25: Courtesy of the author

pages 135, 136, 145, 157: TM & © 2016 Columbia Pictures Industries, Inc. All Rights Reserved.

page 22: Shutterstock/Lario Tus

pages 32, 42: Shutterstock/agsandrew

page 58: Shutterstock/Heartland Arts

page 70: Shutterstock/Andrey-Popov

page 84: Shutterstock/Stepan Kapl

page 96: (composite) Shutterstock/Perseo Medusa and Shutterstock/agsandrew

page 104: Shutterstock/Fer Gregory

page 126: Shutterstock/PhotoProRo

page 140: Shutterstock/Perfect Lazybones

page 148: Shutterstock/Alexander Raths

page 158: Shutterstock/Bruce Rolff

Boxes, torn-paper background: Shutterstock/TADDEUS

About the Authors

Erin Gilbert, Ph.D., M.S., previously taught theoretical physics at Columbia University before taking permanent extended leave to cofound the Ghostbusters. The former academic firebrand's work has been published in *Scientific American*, *Nature*, and *The Journal of Unexplained Things, Explained*. Erin has been friends—and, for a short time, frenemies—with Abby for nearly three decades. As a wise man once said, "There is no spirit more powerful than the spirit of friendship."

Abby L. Yates, Ph.D., is a supernatural scientist and founding member of the Ghostbusters. Prior to joining the private sector, she was a professor of paranormal studies at the Kenneth P. Higgins Institute of Science. She is a fan of *The X-Files*, mid- to late-nineties hip-hop and R&B, and *Blossom*. Her philosophy is that if she can be a scientist, then so can anyone.

Andrew Shaffer is the *New York Times* bestselling author of the essential survival guide *How to Survive a Sharknado and Other Unnatural Disasters*. He is a member of the American Society for Psychical Research and the Horror Writers Association.

Excerpt from Erin and Abby's Forthcoming Book,

A Glimpse into the Unknown: A Journey into a Portal; Catching Sight of the Other Dimension: Discovering the Undiscoverable: A Curiosity Piqued and Peaked

A GLIMPSE INTO THE UNKNOWN.

A journey into a portal.

Catching sight of the other dimension.

Discovering the undiscoverable.

A curiosity piqued *and* peaked.

Such were the titles we considered for this, our second book. So monumental was the subject matter, however, that we had no choice but to use them all.

No longer are we figuratively haunted by ghosts from our past. As the recent outbreak of spectral activity in New York City demonstrates, the ghosts from our past are quite literal. We told some people we wouldn't talk about what happened, but the dangers posed by malevolent entities are clear and unambiguous. What happened in New York City is only the tip of the figurative iceberg when it comes to the threats that lie beyond this world. And we're not talking about figurative iceberg lettuce, either. Or literal iceberg lettuce. We're talking about the type of iceberg that sunk the *Titanic* and turned Leonardo DiCaprio at his most innocent into a human popsicle.

Yet a glimmer of hope exists. Not for DiCaprio's Jack Dawson, but for humanity.

We didn't just have a near-death experience—we also had a near-life experience. The implications of what we've seen go far beyond strengthening the barrier to prevent malevolent forces from entering our dimension. We're on the cusp of a world in which the paranormal is treated not as a sideshow but as a branch of physics worthy of legitimate scientific pursuit. In this new world, death is not the end. It is merely a new frontier.

"There is no death!" poet Henry Wadsworth Longfellow wrote. "What seems so is transition." If dear old Hank Wadsworth had seen what we've seen, he wouldn't have settled for a single exclamation point. HE WOULD HAVE USED AT LEAST THREE!!!—MAYBE FOUR!!!!—AND THEN CAPITALIZED AND <u>UNDERLINED THE ENTIRE POEM</u>.

What did we see on the other side? What was it that so piqued (*and* peaked) our curiosity? We'll tell you! IT WAS MORE MIND-BLOWING THAN QUANTUM ENTANGLEMENT THEORY. IT ELECTRIFIED US MORE THAN TOUCHING THE THIRD RAIL. IT BROUGHT MORE TEARS TO OUR EYES THAN *TITANIC*. WHAT WE'RE ABOUT TO TELL YOU WILL CHANGE THE WAY YOU LOOK AT THE WORLD. WHAT WE SAW WAS—

End of excerpt.